Three Gifts of Love

Stories Adapted by
Jacqueline Mehrabi

Illustrations by
Lisa Jackson

BRILLIANT
BOOKS

Text in 12 pt. Skia
Printed on 100 gram Offset
by Acco, Leuven, Belgium

ISBN 90-5721-033-9
D/2004/7680/03

Brilliant Books
Leuven, Belgium

The Love of ‘Abdu’l-Bahá

Contents

"Blessed, doubly blessed,
is the ground which His footsteps have trodden …
the heart that hath tasted
the sweetness of His love."
Bahá'u'lláh

1

A Festival

Among the mountains and valleys in the north of Persia many flocks of sheep grazed. 'Abdu'l-Bahá's Father, Bahá'u'lláh, owned some of these sheep, which were looked after by shepherds.

Once a year, the shepherds held a festival. When 'Abdu'l-Bahá was about seven years old, He was taken to one of these festivals by a servant called Rahím. Rahím worked for Bahá'u'lláh and looked after the shepherds to make sure they were well and happy.

Rahím took 'Abdu'l-Bahá out into the countryside and up a mountain, which had a flat grassy area on the top. 'Abdu'l-Bahá gazed at the sight before Him. He saw thousands of sheep, as well as cows and goats. There were large bonfires and the appetising smell of cooking. Children were playing games and the shepherds were dressed in their most colourful clothes. 'Abdu'l-Bahá rode over to join them.

The shepherds sang folk songs and danced around the fires all morning, until the food was cooked. Then everyone sat on the grass and had a feast.

When it was time for 'Abdu'l-Bahá to return home, the shepherds gathered round to say goodbye. Rahím told 'Abdu'l-Bahá that they were expecting a gift. Whenever Bahá'u'lláh visited them, He always gave them something. They expected that His Son would do the same. But 'Abdu'l-Bahá had not brought anything with Him and He did not know what to do. He thought for a moment. Then He had an idea. He gave to each shepherd a few sheep from the flocks they were looking after for His Father.

The shepherds were very pleased. When Bahá'u'lláh heard what had happened He was also pleased. He laughed and said, "We must appoint a guardian to protect the Master ... else, some day, He may give Himself away!"

2

Visiting the Prison

A black man with a small boy hurried by. They did not look to left or right but kept their eyes straight ahead, not wanting to draw attention to themselves. It was not a safe time to be walking in the streets. People were being arrested for the smallest thing and everyone was nervous. The followers of the Báb were being arrested and either killed or thrown into prison. The boy was on His way to see His own Father, who had been shut in an underground dungeon known as the Siyáh Chál, or Black Pit, because He believed in the Báb.

The boy was 'Abdu'l-Bahá. The man was Isfandiyar. Isfandiyar had been a loyal and much-loved servant in the house of Bahá'u'lláh. Then Bahá'u'lláh had been arrested and put in prison and thieves had broken into the house and stolen everything. Even then, Isfandiyar had not deserted the Family. He had stayed nearby to pay any debts owed to the shopkeepers, although it was dangerous. 'Abdu'l-Bahá's mother kept telling Isfandiyar to run away and hide before the mob found him and killed him, but he wouldn't. He loved the Family and wanted to help.

When 'Abdu'l-Bahá had asked to be taken to see His Father, Bahá'u'lláh, Isfandiyar said he would take Him.

'Abdu'l-Bahá and Isfandiyar were getting close to the prison. The King's palace was nearby and it looked strange to see such a rich building so close to such a terrible place. They came to a yard where a door led into the underground cell. A guard opened the door and they went inside.

Isfandiyar carried 'Abdu'l-Bahá on his shoulders down two of the steep, dark steps. Suddenly, they heard Bahá'u'lláh's voice coming out of the blackness, saying they should not come any further. The cell was crowded with murderers and thieves and no place for a small boy to be, especially one as tender-hearted and loving as 'Abdu'l-Bahá.

Isfandiyar carried 'Abdu'l-Bahá back up the steps and out into the sunlight, where they waited in the yard.

After a while, the guard led Bahá'u'lláh and the other prisoners out for their daily exercise. Bahá'u'lláh was chained to another prisoner and looked so ill that 'Abdu'l-Bahá fainted. Isfandiyar tenderly carried Him home to His mother and little brother and sister.

A few month's later, Bahá'u'lláh was released from prison, and the Family was sent away from Persia to live in Iráq. 'Abdu'l-Bahá heart was full of joy because He was with His beloved Father again.

And He never forgot Isfandiyar. He told the friends many years later:

"He was the essence of love ... luminous with light. Whenever I think of Isfandiyar, I am moved to tears, although he passed away fifty years ago."

3

The Thorn-Picker

A desert boy was standing on the corner of the street in Baghdád. He was leaning against the wall and his eyes were closed. On his back was a large bundle of thorns. He had been walking all night to come to market to sell them. He was so tired that when he stopped walking he fell asleep still standing up.

People used to buy the thorns to burn on their fires. The bakers burnt them in their stoves when they made bread. The nomads in the desert sometimes used them to make a fence to surround their tents. Then, when it became too hot in the middle of the day, they would pour water over the fence of thorns. As the hot desert wind blew through the wet thorns, it made a cool and pleasant breeze.

The thorns grew in the desert and they were very difficult to pick because they were prickly. Nobody paid much money for them and all the thorn-pickers were poor.

One day, when He was about sixteen years old, 'Abdu'l-Bahá walked through the town of Baghdád and out into the desert. It was the hottest time of day and most people were resting in their houses. But 'Abdu'l-Bahá walked for hours across the scorching desert sand. He had been invited to the home of one of the thorn-pickers and He did not want to disappoint him.

'Abdu'l-Bahá walked for twelve miles before He arrived at a small hut out in the the desert. The thorn-picker was overjoyed to see Him. Although the family had very little food, his wife began to bake a cake for 'Abdu'l-Bahá. She became so excited at having a visitor that she left the cake in the oven too long and it burnt. But 'Abdu'l-Bahá did not mind. He knew that she had tried her best to make Him welcome.

'Abdu'l-Bahá never minded whether a person was rich or poor. To Him it did not matter if they lived in a castle or a hut. What was important was that their hearts were pure. The poor thorn-picker and his wife had pure hearts. That is why 'Abdu'l-Bahá enjoyed being with them.

At the end of the day, 'Abdu'l-Bahá walked the twelve miles back to Baghdád.

4

The House of Happiness

Bahá'u'lláh and His Family were sent further and further away from Persia until they ended up in the grey prison-city of 'Akká. Bahá'u'lláh loved the countryside and one day sadly remarked that He had not seen any green grass or trees for nine years.

"When I heard ... of this saying," said 'Abdu'l-Bahá, "I realised that He was longing for the country, and I was sure that whatever I could do towards the carrying out of His wish would be successful."

But there was a problem. 'Abdu'l-Bahá was also a prisoner within the grey stone walls of 'Akká and, like His Father, was not allowed to leave.

'Abdu'l-Bahá prayed and put His trust in God. First of all, He went to see a man who lived in 'Akká but also owned a beautiful house in the country. The house was called Mazra'ih, which means farm. 'Abdu'l-Bahá had heard that it was surrounded by trees and flowers and a sparkling stream ran through the garden.

The man was not friendly to the Bahá'ís, but 'Abdu'l-Bahá went to visit him anyway and asked him why he was not living in his beautiful country mansion.

"I am an invalid and cannot leave the city," replied the man. "If I go there it is lonely and I am cut off from my friends."

"While you are not living there and the place is empty, let it to us," suggested 'Abdu'l-Bahá.

The man was surprised. After all, 'Abdu'l-Bahá was a prisoner and did not have permission to leave the town. However, he agreed to let the house and 'Abdu'l-Bahá gave Him money for the rent.

'Abdu'l-Bahá immediately sent workmen to repair the house, put in a bath, and tidy the garden. But He still had not seen it for Himself.

One day He decided to try to leave the prison city, which was surrounded by a high, thick stone wall. He walked towards the enormous gate that led out of the city. Soldiers were on guard on either side of the gate to prevent any prisoners from leaving, but they allowed 'Abdu'l-Bahá to walk through. He went out of the city again the next day, and still nobody stopped Him.

When the work on the mansion was finished, 'Abdu'l-Bahá went to Bahá'u'lláh. He said that the mansion was now ready and there was a carriage waiting to drive Him there. At first, Bahá'u'lláh said He could not go because He was still a prisoner. 'Abdu'l-Bahá asked the head Muslim religious leader of the city to beg Bahá'u'lláh to leave. This man had once been an enemy of Bahá'u'lláh but now loved Him very much. He knelt down before Him and said he would not move until Bahá'u'lláh agreed to go!

Eventually, Bahá'u'lláh laughed and agreed. As He left the dull and dirty city, the soldiers at the gate did nothing to stop Him.

From the mansion, Bahá'u'lláh could see far across the fields to the distant mountains. The wind danced in the tops of the tall, green trees and the garden was full of oranges. He lived there for the next two years and the house became known as "The House of Happiness".

5

The Paradise Garden

'Abdu'l-Bahá left Bahá'u'lláh in the Mansion of Mazra'ih and returned to the city of 'Akká. Here, He spent His time looking after the friends and the poor people in the city. He also met with the town officials and they began to realise that Bahá'ís were good people who believed in God. Through getting to know 'Abdu'l-Bahá, they became more helpful and kind. 'Abdu'l-Bahá longed to be with Bahá'u'lláh, but He knew He could help Him best by staying in 'Akká.

At this time 'Abdu'l-Bahá also made a lovely garden for Bahá'u'lláh to visit. In the middle there was a fountain, which splashed and sparkled in the sunshine. Bahá'u'lláh called it the Ridván, or Paradise, Garden because it was so peaceful.

Bahá'u'lláh often stayed in a summer house in the Ridván Garden. He would invite the children and the friends who lived in 'Akká to come for picnics in the garden, and they spent many happy times together.

Because of the love of 'Abdu'l-Bahá, Bahá'u'lláh could now rest beneath leafy mulberry trees, surrounded by fragrant flowers.

6
The Rich Merchant

A Persian merchant who was living in Egypt had recently become a Bahá'í, and he longed to visit Bahá'u'lláh. He wrote a letter asking for permission to go on pilgrimage to `Akká to see Him. Bahá'u'lláh gave permission, but said that first the merchant must pay back all the money he owed to other people. He was only rich because he had not paid his bills!

It took the merchant five years to pay all his debts. By the time he had done this he was poor and had hardly any money left. He just had enough to pay for food for his family while he was away and for a cheap ticket for the boat journey to visit Bahá'u'lláh.

Bahá'u'lláh sent one of the Bahá'ís to the port of Haifa to meet the boat. The believer looked for a rich merchant dressed in fine clothes and carrying expensive luggage, but he did not see anyone who looked like that. He returned to `Akká and told Bahá'u'lláh that the pilgrim was not on the boat.

But Bahá'u'lláh knew the merchant had arrived, so this time He sent `Abdu'l-Bahá to find him.

Meanwhile, the merchant was feeling very sorry for himself. He had waited five years to see Bahá'u'lláh. He had spent all his money paying his bills and debts. He did not even have a woollen coat to keep himself warm. Even the small shawl he had wrapped round his shoulders had slipped off and fallen into the sea as he walked over the gangplank to the boat. He was only dressed in cotton clothes and was cold and unhappy.

And, to top it all, it seemed that nobody was at the pier to meet him!

He was sitting huddled on a bench feeling very sorry for himself when `Abdu'l-Bahá arrived. At once `Abdu'l-Bahá knew that the lonely looking man was the pilgrim they were expecting. He walked up to the merchant and explained what had happened. The merchant was happy to see 'Abdu'l-Bahà but he did not feel ready to go to `Akkà just yet. He wanted to feel peaceful and happy when he met Bahá'u'lláh, not cross and complaining. He knew he needed to say many prayers before he was ready.

`Abdu'l-Bahá understood. He sat down on the bench next to the unhappy man and wrapped half of His own cloak around him to keep him warm. They sat on the bench all night saying prayers together. By the time morning came, the pilgrim's heart was full of love and `Abdu'l-Bahá took him to Bahá'u'lláh.

7

Na`úm

Every Friday, over a hundred poor people came to the house of 'Abdu'l-Bahá. They would gather in the garden and 'Abdu'l-Bahá would speak to each one, giving them money or advising them where to find work. Sometimes His hands became scratched and bruised because the people held onto them so tightly.

Each week a poor, crippled woman called Na`úm came to see Him. She had no family to look after her and was too old to work. 'Abdu'l-Bahá always spoke to her kindly and gave her money to buy food.

One day a man came running to 'Abdu'l-Bahá. "Oh, Master," he said, "that poor Na`úm has measles.... Everyone is keeping away from her. What can be done about her?"

'Abdu'l-Bahá immediately rented a room for Na`úm and gave her His own bed to sleep on. Then He paid a woman to look after her. He sent food to Na`úm every day and made sure she was comfortable and clean until the day she died.

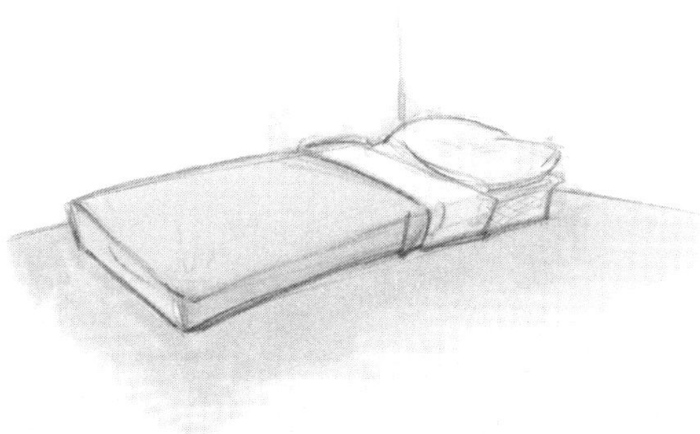

8

The Angry Shaykh

Most of the people in 'Akká knew that the Bahá'ís were honest and kind. But there was one man who hated them. His name was Shaykh Mahmúd. He was a Muslim and did not understand that the Bahá'ís were good people who believed in God.

One day at a meeting people were saying how kind 'Abdu'l-Bahá was, and the Shaykh became very angry. He stamped out the room and rushed to a mosque where He knew he would find 'Abdu'l-Bahá praying.

He took hold of 'Abdu'l-Bahá and shook Him roughly. 'Abdu'l-Bahá remained very calm. He looked at the Shaykn and lovingly reminded him that the Prophet Muhammad had said we should be kind to a guest, even if he is not a believer.

Shaykh Mahmúd turned away, feeling ashamed. He knew that 'Abdu'l-Bahá was right. He ran to his house and locked the door.

A few days later he came out of his house and went to 'Abdu'l-Bahá. He asked to be forgiven for his bad behaviour. And he became a Bahá'í.

9

The Sick Man

A man who lived in the same street as 'Abdu'l-Bahá in 'Akká became very ill. He had a disease called tuberculosis, and everyone was afraid of catching it. His friends stayed away, and even his family did not like to go into his bedroom to help him. A servant left his food just inside the door, and the ill man hardly had the strength to reach it.

Through the window of the house, 'Abdu'l-Bahá's sister saw what was happening and told 'Abdu'l-Bahá. At once He went to the sick man's house. He was not afraid of the disease and felt sorry for the man. He sat and talked with him for hours so that he would not be lonely. He took him little treats to eat and read him stories.

The man became weaker and weaker, but still his family and friends would not come near him. But 'Abdu'l-Bahá visited him every day, and when he died, 'Abdu'l-Bahá was with him.

10

The Unfriendly Afghan

There was a very unhappy man who lived in 'Akká. He was called "the Afghan" because he came from a country called Afghanistan.

He was not friendly to 'Abdu'l-Bahá. He would stand up in the mosque and tell the people not to have anything to do with Him. But 'Abdu'l-Bahá was always friendly to him.

The Afghan was poor, and he was often cold and hungry. 'Abdu'l-Bahá would send him food and warm clothes. The Afghan always accepted the things 'Abdu'l-Bahá sent but never said thank you.

Once, when the Afghan was ill, 'Abdu'l-Bahá took a doctor to see him and give him medicine. The Afghan held out his arm so the doctor could take his pulse. At the same time, he covered his head with his cloak and turned his face away so that he did not have to see 'Abdu'l-Bahá.

Many years passed by. During all this time 'Abdu'l-Bahá sent food and clothes and money and medicine to the unfriendly Afghan. And the Afghan continued to say bad things about 'Abdu'l-Bahá.

One day there was a knock on 'Abdu'l-Bahá's door. And there was the Afghan. He was crying bitterly. He fell to the ground at the feet of 'Abdu'l-Bahá.

"Forgive me, Sir!" he cried. "For twenty-four years I have done evil to you. For twenty-four years you have done good to me. Now I know I have been in the wrong."

'Abdu'l-Bahá gently told the Afghan to stand up, and they became friends.

11

'Abdu'l-Bahá's Grandchild

It was early in the morning and 'Abdu'l-Bahá was sitting by the window writing letters. A samovar bubbled away in the corner and a young girl was busy making tea. 'Abdu'l-Bahá put down His pen and asked one of the Bahá'ís to chant a prayer.

She had just finished when a little boy appeared in the doorway. He was 'Abdu'l-Bahá's grandson Shoghi Effendi. He took off his shoes and quietly came into the room.

Shoghi Effendi did not look at the other people in the room. He looked straight at 'Abdu'l-Bahá. 'Abdu'l-Bahá looked back at Shoghi Effendi, and His eyes were full of love.

The small boy slowly walked towards 'Abdu'l-Bahá and stood in front of Him. Still looking at 'Abdu'l-Bahá, he reached down and picked up the hem of his Grandfather's robe. He lifted it to his forehead, kissed it, and gently put it down again.

'Abdu'l-Bahá nodded and smiled. There was no need for words. Shoghi Effendi knew how much 'Abdu'l-Bahá loved him. He turned and ran happily out of the room to play.

When 'Abdu'l-Bahá's little grandson grew up, he became the Guardian of the Bahá'í Faith.

12

The Wild-Looking Woman

A wild-looking young woman came towards 'Abdu'l-Bahá. She was the daughter of a desert chief and had once been rich and powerful, but now she was poor and had fallen on hard times. She looked as though she would fight anyone who displeased her!

A young pilgrim from America was with 'Abdu'l-Bahá at the time. When she saw the woman she was frightened and wanted to run away. She watched in fear as the woman came up to 'Abdu'l-Bahá.

The wild-looking woman stopped in front of 'Abdu'l-Bahá and bowed her head. 'Abdu'l-Bahá knew her. He spoke to her gently and pressed a coin into her hand. Her face lit up and she thanked Him again and again.

"I will pray for you!" she said.

"Thank you," said 'Abdu'l-Bahá.

13

The Poor Fisherwoman

'Abdu'l-Bahá set off to travel round the bay to Haifa. He climbed into a horse-drawn carriage, which was full of poor people with their bags and belongings.

The driver was surprised when he saw 'Abdu'l-Bahá. "Your Excellency surely wishes a private carriage!" he said.

"No," replied 'Abdu'l-Bahá, to the surprise of the driver, who thought that someone as important as 'Abdu'l-Bahá should be riding in a more comfortable carriage.

The horses pulled the carriage over the sandy beach, which at the time was the only way to travel to Haifa as there was no proper road. The waves washed over the horses' hooves as they trotted along the shore. When they arrived in Haifa, the driver reigned in the horses and waited for everyone to get off.

At that moment, a poor fisherwoman came up to 'Abdu'l-Bahá. She looked very sad and said that she had not been able to catch any fish all day and had nothing to take home for her hungry children.

'Abdu'l-Bahá gave her money to buy food.

"You now see the reason why I would not take a private carriage," He said to the driver, who had been watching as all this happened. "Why should I ride in luxury when so many are starving?"

14

Beloved of God

In 1898, a group of pilgrims from America went to the Holy Land. One evening 'Abdu'l-Bahá told them that there would be a special meeting the following Sunday. The meeting was to be held under a group of cypress trees on Mount Carmel. 'Abdu'l-Bahá had sat with Bahá'u'lláh under these trees.

That night everyone was very happy when they went to bed, thinking about the meeting. But the next morning one of pilgrims, whose name was May, woke up with a fever. She was so ill she could not get out of bed.

'Abdu'l-Bahá came to see her. He held her hands and then He felt her forehead. She was very hot and had a temperature, and 'Abdu'l-Bahá said she should stay in bed.

When Sunday came, May was still unwell. 'Abdu'l-Bahá felt her pulse and said , "There will be no meeting on Mount Carmel today ... we could not go and leave one of the beloved of God alone and sick.... We could none of us be happy unless all the beloved are happy."

15

The First American Believer

Thornton Chase became a Bahá'í in 1894, just two years after Bahá'u'lláh died. 'Abdu'l-Bahá said he was the first American believer.

Mr Chase visited 'Abdu'l-Bahá in 'Akká in 1907, but there was trouble in the Holy Land at the time and he was only able to stay four days. Mr Chase wept when he had to leave, but cheered up when 'Abdu'l-Bahá told him that they would meet again.

Five years later, a message came to say that 'Abdu'l-Bahá was coming to America. Mr Chase was very excited. But while 'Abdu'l-Bahá was on His way to America, Mr Chase became ill and died.

When 'Abdu'l-Bahá heard the sad news, He made a special trip to the cemetery where Mr Chase was buried. When He got off the train, He took a tram out to the cemetery. It was very beautiful, with tall trees and many flowers. He leant against a tree in silence for a while looking at the grave. He asked for some flowers, which He lovingly laid on the grave, and chanted prayers for the pure soul of Mr Chase on its journey through all the worlds of God.

"The people will honour this grave," said 'Abdu'l-Bahá. "Therefore the friends of God must visit this grave and on my behalf bring flowers...."

Then he knelt down and kissed the grave of this dear believer.

So, in a way, Thornton Chase did meet 'Abdu'l-Bahá a second time after all.

16

A Newspaper Reporter

Kate was a newspaper reporter in America and she was going to see 'Abdu'l-Bahá. She did not know what to expect as she walked through the front door of the hotel and up to the top floor. She rang the bell and it opened almost immediately.

The room was full of people and Kate sat down and waited Soon 'Abdu'l-Bahá came in. He spoke to everyone in turn, and patted the cheeks of an old man and a youth with a rosy face When he came to Kate, he gently patted her cheek too!

Kate had a long talk with 'Abdu'l-Bahá and asked Him many questions. 'Abdu'l-Bahá said that if we obey God and are good and kind, then we will always be happy. He also told her that she must think seriously about what He said, and to be truthfu when she wrote about her visit to Him. He then said He had to leave to meet some poor people. He invited Kate to go with Him

He held Kate's hand as they walked out of the building to a car waiting outside. The driver of the car took them to a place called the Bowery Mission where four hundred poor men were waiting. Most of the men had nowhere to live and often slept outside on park benches or on the streets or under bridges.

'Abdu'l-Bahá knew what it felt like to be poor. When He wa eight years old, His Father, Bahá'u'lláh, had been put in prison because He believed in the new teachings the Báb had brough from God. During that difficult time 'Abdu'l-Bahá and Hi brother and sister had often been cold and hungry as there wa no money to buy food.

When 'Abdu'l-Bahá and Kate arrived at the Bowery Mission, He spoke to the poor men who were gathered there.

"Tonight I am very happy," 'Abdu'l-Bahá told them, "for I have come here to meet my friends."

At the end of His talk, He said, "I ask you to accept 'Abdu'l-Bahá as your servant."

Before He left, He gave each man money to pay for somewhere warm and safe to sleep that night.

Later, when Kate was writing an article about her meeting with 'Abdu'l-Bahá, she said that her last view of Him was "as he stood at the head of the Bowery Mission line … giving to each a bit of silver and a word of blessing".

17

17

The Chambermaid

'Abdu'l-Bahá had been talking to the poor people in the Bowery Mission in New York. When he left, He had given each one a piece of silver. But He still had some coins left in a bag.

When 'Abdu'l-Bahá returned to the hotel where He was staying, He saw one of the chambermaids who cleaned the bedrooms. He knew she was not paid very much for all her hard work. He told her to hold out her apron – and to her amazement He filled it with all the money left in the bag.

When someone told her how 'Abdu'l-Bahá had given His money away to the poor men in the Bowery Mission, she said she would give her money away too.

Later that day, she knocked on the door of 'Abdu'l-Bahá's room. She knew that He was leaving the next day and she wanted to say goodbye. She was sad that He was leaving and her eyes were full of tears. The room was full of people but she did not look at them – she walked straight up to 'Abdu'l-Bahá.

"I wanted to say goodbye, sir," she said shyly, "and to thank you for all your goodness to me. I never expected such goodness. And to ask you to pray for me."

She begun to cry, then hid her face in her apron and ran out of the room.

18

A Black Rose

'Abdu'l-Bahá was on His way to a meeting. As He walked down the street, a group of boys began to follow Him. Because He came from another country and was dressed differently, some of them became cheeky and even began to throw sticks at Him.

One of the Bahá'ís went to talk to them. She explained how 'Abdu'l-Bahá was a very kind and holy person. The boys became quiet. Then they asked if they could go with 'Abdu'l-Bahá to the meeting. She said that was not possible but if they came to her house the following Sunday, she would arrange for them to meet 'Abdu'l-Bahá there.

She did not think the boys would come, but the next Sunday almost thirty of them turned up. They were all very poor but they had tried to make themselves clean and smart.

The boys trooped into the room where 'Abdu'l-Bahá was waiting for them. He shook their hands, put His arm around their shoulders, and welcomed them with smiles and laughter.

'Abdu'l-Bahá was especially kind to a boy at the end of the line. The boy had held back, not knowing whether he would be welcomed or not. 'Abdu'l-Bahá smiled even more warmly when He saw the boy and said, "Here is a black rose!"

Everyone looked at the boy. His face was shining with love and happiness. He was used to being bullied and called all sorts of names, but he had never before been called a black rose!

'Abdu'l-Bahá opened a large box of chocolates. He went round giving a handful to each boy. He picked one of the chocolates from the box and placed it against the cheek of the black boy.

'Abdu'l-Bahá looked at the other boys. He did not say anything, but they knew what He meant. He was telling them that this black brother of theirs was not only beautiful like a rose, but he was also good and sweet like a chocolate!

19

Ragged Trousers

It was early in the morning and 'Abdu'l-Bahá was walking up and down the pavement outside the hotel dictating letters to His secretary. There were no other people about, except for a tramp who was walking slowly up the street towards Him.

'Abdu'l-Bahá noticed that the old man's clothes were torn and dirty. His trousers were so full of holes they hardly covered his legs and were useless for keeping him warm.

'Abdu'l-Bahá smiled at the old man. He held his hand and tried to cheer him up. After a while a faint smile appeared on the grey, tired face. 'Abdu'l-Bahá looked at the man's ragged trousers and said that something needed to be done about them! He stepped into the shadow of a nearby porch and took off His own trousers, which He wore beneath a long cloak, and gave them to the old man.

"May God go with you," said 'Abdu'l-Bahá.

Then He turned back to His secretary and continued to dictate letters as though nothing unusual had happened.

20

The Stone that was Thrown Away

It was decided to build a Temple in America. The Bahá'ís began to save their money to give to a fund so that work could begin. But there was one poor woman who did not have any money to give. Her name was Nettie. She wished with all her heart that she too could give something to help build the Temple.

First of all, a piece of land was bought in a beautiful spot near a river. A meeting was arranged on the land, and the friends were invited to gather there to say prayers. 'Abdu'l-Bahá was also going to be present to bless the spot where the Temple was going to be built.

Nettie wanted to go too, but she felt sad that she had nothing to give. Then she remembered seeing a builder's yard near her home. She went to the yard and asked the owner if he would give her a stone.

"Help yourself," said the builder, pointing to the pile of stones. They were all odd shapes and were going to be thrown away because they were not the right shape for building walls.

Nettie chose a large stone, but it was too heavy for her to carry. So she went home and fetched an old pram and put the stone in it. Then, with the help of another Bahá'í, she took it on three bus journeys until she came near to the Temple land. The bus drivers were not too pleased at having a pram with a rock in it on their buses!

When Nettie and her friend got off the last bus and were pushing the pram over a broken bit of pavement, it fell to pieces!

Nettie looked at the broken pram in despair and thought she would never get to the meeting in time. Then some boys came by with a wagon and they offered to help.

By the time Nettie arrived at the Temple land it was late and the prayers had already begun. But when 'Abdu'l-Bahá saw the stone He smiled. When the prayers were finished, He said that that was the stone He wanted to lay as the corner stone for the Temple.

A hole was dug and the stone laid in it. Then 'Abdu'l-Bahá put earth round the stone and patted it down so that it was firmly held in the ground.

The builders had not wanted the stone because it was an odd shape. But 'Abdu'l-Bahá chose it because Nettie had given it with love. Later, a beautiful Temple was built on that spot.

21

'Abdu'l-Bahá's Spiritual Children

There was a buzz of excitement in the air. 'Abdu'l-Bahá had come to Chicago and there was to be a special meeting with the children. Some of the children lived outside the town. They had to get up at five o'clock in the morning to get to the meeting in time.

When everyone arrived, the children sat in a circle. The grown-ups sat behind them.

'Abdu'l-Bahá entered the room and everyone stood up. Then the children sung a song they had been practising. It was called "Softly His Voice is Calling Now". When they finished, 'Abdu'l-Bahá spoke to each of the children and asked them what their names were. He gently stroked their hair and held their hands, and kissed the little ones.

One very small child ran up to 'Abdu'l-Bahá and threw herself into His arms. He gave her a hug, and when He let her go, she stood for moment looking at Him. Then she laughed out loud in happiness. All the other children began laughing too.

"You are all my children," said 'Abdu'l-Bahá, "you are my spiritual children ... you are very dear; you are most beloved!"

There were some flowers on the table. 'Abdu'l-Bahá picked them up and divided them among the children. He also gave each child an envelope full of sweet-smelling rose petals.

Then He invited them to come outside into a park to have their photographs taken with Him.

22

The Old Watchman

It was a very hot day. In the afternoon everyone expected that 'Abdu'l-Bahá would rest. But He said He wished to go to the Natural History Museum. The believers could not understand why He wanted to go out when it was so hot.

They walked with Him through the city. There were no trees to shade them from the sun. At last they came within sight of the museum. 'Abdu'l-Bahá sat down on a stone ledge to rest, feeling very tired.

One of the Bahá'ís, who was called Juliet, offered to find out if there was a door nearby which led into the museum so that 'Abdu'l-Bahá would not have to walk all the way up to the main entrance. Eventually, she found a watchman, who looked after the grounds. He was a Jew, very old and bent and with a kind face. He said that all the other doors were locked, but they could take a short-cut over the grass to the main door.

The watchman led the way and 'Abdu'l-Bahá and the friends went into the museum. In one room they saw a huge whale hanging from the ceiling. In another room there was some art from Mexico and lovely Persian bracelets.

'Abdu'l-Bahá decided not to go into the rest of the rooms and returned to the front door and went out into the garden. He sat down on the grass beneath a tree. The Bahá'ís stood around, wondering what was going to happen next.

The old watchman reappeared.

"Is He tired?" he whispered, looking at 'Abdu'l-Bahá. "Who is He? He looks like such a great man. I would like to speak to Him."

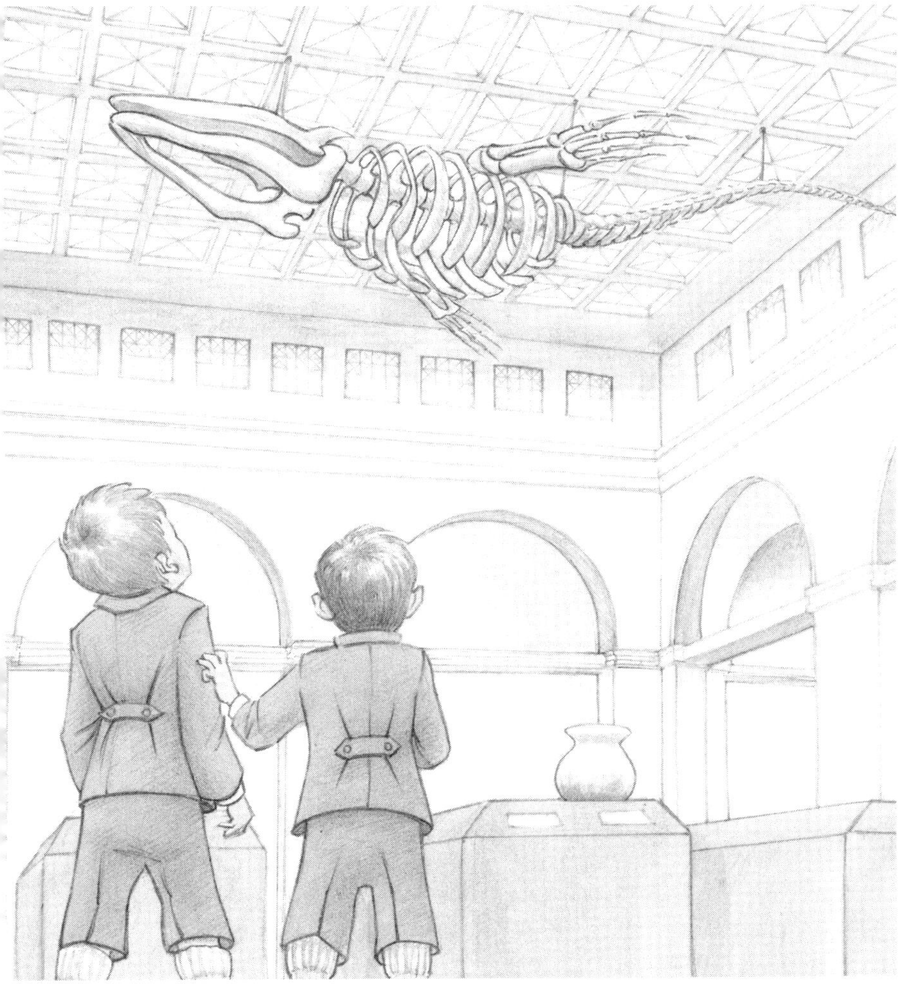

Juliet took the watchman to ʽAbdu'l-Bahá. ʽAbdu'l-Bahá's eyes were bright and kind as He looked at the old watchman.

"Come and sit by Me," He said.

The watchman said he was not allowed to sit on the grass, so ʽAbdu'l-Bahá stood up and they talked together.

"You didn't see the whole of the museum," said the watchman. "You didn't go up to the third floor. The fossils and birds are up there."

ʽAbdu'l-Bahá smiled. "I am tired of travelling and looking at the things of this world," He said. "I want to go above and travel and see in the next world." He gave the watchman a big smile. "What do you think about that?"

The watchman told ʽAbdu'l-Bahá that he did not want to die and leave this world. ʽAbdu'l-Bahá told him that there was no need to be worried. He said that this world is like a room in a house. Going to the next world is just like going upstairs.

"Oh I see!" said the watchman happily. "I see!"

✣ ✣ ✣ ✣ ✣

But that is not the end of the story. When Juliet and everyone else returned home, she wished she had invited the watchman to one of the Bahá'í meetings. A week later she went back by herself to the museum to invite him to come.

When she arrived, she could not find him anywhere. Instead, there was a young watchman looking after the grounds. Juliet asked him where the old man was, but he did not know anything about him.

Then Juliet guessed what had happened. After their visit the week before, the old watchman must have died. And that was why ʽAbdu'l-Bahá had gone to the museum. It wasn't because He wanted to see the whale or Persian bracelets. He wanted to see the old watchman and tell him that he did not need to be afraid of dying.

23

Mona

Mona looked at 'Abdu'l-Bahá. He was dressed in dazzling white. His turban was pushed back a little from His face. His blue eyes twinkled. He looked at her and smiled. Then He reached down and lifted her up.

Little Mona felt warm and safe in the arms of 'Abdu'l-Bahá. He kissed her on both cheeks.

"Are you French or English?" He asked her.

Mona was too shy to answer. 'Abdu'l-Bahá smiled again.

"If the people ask you whether you are English or French," He said, "tell them you are a Bahá'í!"

24

Love of the Kingdom

Stanwood Cobb was a school teacher. He met 'Abdu'l-Bahá many times. The first time, Mr Cobb was not sure what to do.

"I wonder if I should shake 'Abdu'l-Bahá's hand?" he thought.

While he stood there hesitating, 'Abdu'l-Bahá came towards him, took him in His arms, and gave him a big hug.

"You are welcome!" said 'Abdu'l-Bahá.

✧ ✧ ✧ ✧ ✧

Another time, Stanwood Cobb was ill in bed when he met 'Abdu'l-Bahá. 'Abdu'l-Bahá sent a doctor and also visited Mr Cobb in his room. 'Abdu'l-Bahá said that He wished He was the one who was ill, not Mr Cobb.

"I would that I could take your illness upon myself," He said.

✧ ✧ ✧ ✧ ✧

Yet another time was when 'Abdu'l-Bahá was in America. Stanwood Cobb took his father with him to meet 'Abdul-Bahá. His father was not a Bahá'í, but he was a good man. He just did not understand how wise 'Abdu'l-Bahá was. Instead of listening to 'Abdu'l-Bahá, He spent all the time speaking about his own ideas.

Mr Cobb became upset and embarrassed and thought his father should listen and not talk so much! But 'Abdu'l-Bahá did not mind. He sat and listened to Mr Cobb's father with love and kindness. Mr Cobb's father left feeling very happy.

✧ ✧ ✧ ✧ ✧

Stanwood Cobb also met 'Abdu'l-Bahá in France.

'Abdu'l-Bahá asked him, "What do you teach?"

Mr Cobb replied, "English, Latin, Algebra and Geometry."

'Abdu'l-Bahá's eyes shone as He looked at Mr Cobb. "Do you teach the spiritual things?" He asked.

Mr Cobb did not know what to say. "No," he said at last, "there is no time for that."

'Abdu'l-Bahá was silent. He did not say anything more. He did not criticise Mr Cobb. But Mr Cobb knew that 'Abdu'l-Bahá was telling him it is important to teach spiritual things first, and then the other subjects.

✧ ✧ ✧ ✧ ✧

When Stanwood Cobb met 'Abdu'l-Bahá for the last time, all he remembered afterwards was that 'Abdu'l-Bahá had embraced him, kissed him, and said three times,

"Be on fire with the love of the Kingdom!
Be on fire with the love of the Kingdom!
Be on fire with the love of the Kingdom!"

25

"My Dear One"

The first English person to become a Bahá'í was a young man called Thomas Breakwell. He heard about the Faith when he was on holiday in France. He wrote a letter to 'Abdu'l-Bahá in 'Akká, saying, "My Lord, I believe...."

'Abdu'l-Bahá sent a cable back inviting Thomas to come on pilgrimage to the Holy Land.

While he was on pilgrimage, Thomas told 'Abdu'l-Bahá that he was worried about his job. He worked for a firm that had cotton plantations in the southern states of the United States of America. Thomas was paid a great deal of money for his work. But he was worried because he knew his firm made small children work long hours in the cotton mills and they were not always treated kindly.

'Abdu'l-Bahá advised Thomas to leave his job.

Immediately, Thomas wrote a letter to his firm saying he was not going to work for them any more. 'Abdu'l-Bahá also told him to return to France and teach the Faith there. Thomas obeyed 'Abdu'l-Bahá and when his pilgrimage ended he went to live in Paris.

Thomas had a very pure heart. He was always doing a kindness for other people. Once he was sitting with a friend on a bus in Paris going to a meeting when he looked through the window and saw an old lady struggling to push a heavy cart of apples over a bridge. Thomas said "excuse me" to his friend and got off the bus. He went up to the old lady and helped to push her cart over the bridge to the other side.

One day Thomas became ill. In those days there was not always medicine to cure people. Thomas was in great pain because of his illness but he never complained. In fact, he seemed to get happier every day. During this time, he wrote to ‘Abdu’l-Bahá, Who loved him very much. Without being told, ‘Abdu’l-Bahá knew when Thomas Breakwell died. He wrote a beautiful prayer in his memory. Part of it says:

"O Breakwell, O my dear one! … I shall never forget thee. I pray for thee by day, by night…. O Breakwell, O my dear one!"

26

The Beautiful House

It was four o'clock in the afternoon and a carriage was being driven through the streets of Paris. 'Abdu'l-Bahá was inside the carriage with a few of the Bahá'ís.

They left the wide streets and grand houses where rich people lived, until they came to an area of the town were the streets were very narrow. 'Abdu'l-Bahá was on His way to meet some children in a poor part of Paris.

The meeting was being held by two Bahá'ís called Mr and Mrs Ponsonaille, and they too were poor. Every day they went without their midday meal and instead bought food for the neighbourhood children. The meetings were held in a wooden hut the Ponsonailles had built with planks of wood and nails the local Bahá'ís had given them.

The carriage stopped in a street nearby and 'Abdu'l-Bahá and the other Bahá'ís got out and began to walk down a narrow lane. Mattresses and eiderdowns hung out of the windows of the houses, airing in the afternoon sun. Inside the houses men and women were shouting and fighting. At the end of the lane was the hut.

Inside the hut was a picture of the Greatest Name, and a group of children were singing. They were all ages. The youngest was just a baby and the oldest was fifteen. None of their clothes fitted them properly, but they were all very clean. Among them were some rough boys who were being noisy and wouldn't behave, but they became quiet when 'Abdu'l-Bahá came in.

"I am very glad to be here with you," 'Abdu'l-Bahá told them. "I am very glad to see you all here. I love you very much. I have been in many beautiful houses, but this is more beautiful to me than all the others, for the spirit of the love of Bahá'u'lláh is here."

He turned to Mr and Mrs Ponsonaille. "This is a great work you are doing for the love of God," He told them. "Kings and Queens have never been talked of and remembered as you will be. You are workers in the Kingdom of Abhá and I am very happy and love you very much."

'Abdu'l-Bahá raised His hands and said a prayer. When He finished, the children crowded round and held His hands. As He left the hut, the rough boys fell over each other in their eagerness to be close to Him and hold His hands too.

He began to walk back through the narrow lane to the carriage. People were looking out of every window and doorway, curiously watching Him pass by. A man dressed in rags ran forward to hold open the carriage door for Him.

By this time the crowd was getting a bit out of hand. People began fighting one another in the lane and calling names. A policeman appeared and he helped the rest of the Bahá'ís to safely reach the carriage.

27

The Meeting

'Abdu'l-Bahá was travelling through Germany, Austria and Hungary. It was winter and snowing. 'Abdu'l-Bahá was not used to such wintry weather and He caught a bad cold and could hardly speak. A doctor advised Him not to go out and to try not to speak until He was better. The Bahá'ís in the town where He was staying said prayers asking God to make 'Abdu'l-Bahá better.

Meanwhile, in a hall in another part of the town, people were beginning to gather for a meeting. They had come to hear 'Abdu'l-Bahá. They were disappointed when one of the Bahá'ís explained that 'Abdu'l-Bahá was ill and unable to come and that someone else would give the talk.

Back in His hotel, 'Abdu'l-Bahá knew the friends would be disappointed if He did not turn up. Some of the friends suggested that if He kept warm and travelled to the meeting by car perhaps He could still manage to go. 'Abdu'l-Bahá agreed.

The people in the audience were surprised and delighted when 'Abdu'l-Bahá walked into the hall. And as He began to tell them about Bahá'u'lláh, His voice became stronger and filled the whole hall.

At the end of His talk, 'Abdu'l-Bahá was quickly leaving the room to return to His hotel when He heard someone crying. It was a lady who wanted to get near to Him but couldn't because there were so many people crowding round Him. 'Abdu'l-Bahá immediately turned and went over to talk to her.

The next day, someone asked 'Abdu'l-Bahá how He was feeling. He said He was feeling much better and that going to the meeting had been the best medicine!

28

A Garland of Flowers

Once, when 'Abdu'l-Bahá was intending to catch a train, the friends were puzzled because He was calmly sitting at a table writing letters. His luggage was packed and people were waiting to go with Him to the station. Some of them became worried and said it was time to go, otherwise 'Abdu'l-Bahá would miss the train.

But 'Abdu'l-Bahá just smiled and said, "There are things of more importance than trains!"

The friends were puzzled and did not know what to do.

At that moment a man came running into the house looking for 'Abdu'l-Bahá. He was a follower of the Prophet Zoroaster and had a garland of white flowers in his hand. He had heard about 'Abdu'l-Bahá and had come to see Him. The man bowed and put the garland of flowers around 'Abdu'l-Bahá's neck. Then he anointed everyone in the room with perfume of roses.

Everyone was surprised at the man's strange behaviour. And even more surprised that 'Abdu'l-Bahá had known he was coming.

'Abdu'l-Bahá talked to the man for several minutes and made him very welcome. Then He left just in time to catch the train.

29
The Workman

'Abdu'l-Bahá had just finished giving a talk in a hotel in England. He came out of the room and was walking through the hall when He saw a workman with a bag of tools.

The man worked hard every day so that he could make enough money to feed his family. When he finished work late in the evening he would go home and sleep, too tired to do anything else. He was surprised when 'Abdu'l-Bahá stopped to talk to him.

"I don't know much about religious things," the man admitted sadly, "as I have no time for anything but my work."

"That is good," said 'Abdu'l-Bahá. "Such work is a prayer unto God."

The workman's face lit up. No-one had ever said that to him before. It made him feel very happy.

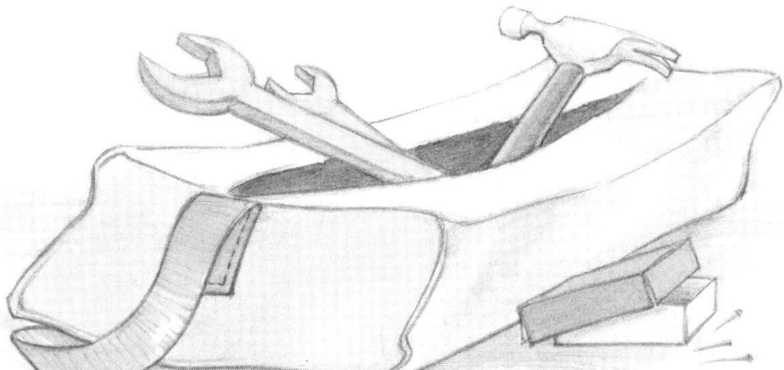

30

The Uninvited Guest

Two ladies arrived to see 'Abdu'l-Bahá. They had been invited to have a meal with Him and some other guests and had travelled all day to get to London. They only had a few hours before they had to get the train home again.

They had been with 'Abdu'l-Bahá for half an hour when a man walked into the room and interrupted their conversation. He was a reporter from a newspaper. He had not been invited and he was not very polite. He sat down and began smoking a cigarette without asking. He then began to talk and talk, not giving 'Abdu'l-Bahá a chance to say anything.

The ladies were shocked at his bad behaviour. And they were cross because he was spoiling their precious time with 'Abdu'-Bahá. They wished he would go away.

Suddenly 'Abdu'l-Bahá got up and beckoned to the reporter to follow Him out of the room. He took the man to His own room, and the ladies were left sitting on their own. They were pleased that the reporter had gone. But so, too, had 'Abdu'l-Bahá!

After a while they heard 'Abdu'l-Bahá's voice outside the room. He was speaking kindly to the reporter as He said good-bye at the front door. 'Abdu'l-Bahá then came back into the room where the guests were waiting.

"Oh Master!" they said.

'Abdu'l-Bahá looked at them sadly.

"You were making that poor man uncomfortable," He said. "I took him away to make him feel happy."

31

The Face in the Newspaper

A tramp was sleeping on the bank of the river Thames. He had no home to go to. Once he had lived a comfortable life. He was well-educated and his father was a clergyman in the Church. But things had gone wrong in his life, and now he was poor and alone and unhappy. In fact, he was so miserable he did not wish to go on living.

The man woke up, feeling cold and hungry. He walked down the street and passed a newspaper shop. It was then that he saw the Face! It was a photograph of 'Abdu'l-Bahá in a newspaper. It seemed to the man that 'Abdu'l-Bahá was looking straight at him and knew how unhappy he was.

The newspaper article said that 'Abdu'l-Bahá was staying at a house in London, and gave the address, which was thirty miles away. Although it took all day, the man walked until he came to the house where 'Abdu'l-Bahá was staying.

When he arrived, the lady who owned the house invited him in and gave him something to eat. When he had rested, he told her about his sad life and then how he had seen the photograph of 'Abdu'l-Bahá.

"He seemed to speak to me, and call me to Him," said the man. "Tell me, is He here? Will He see me? Even me?"

"Of course He will see you!" said the lady. And at that moment 'Abdu'l-Bahá opened the door and came into the room. He stretched out His hands to the man.

"Welcome! Most welcome!" said 'Abdu'l-Bahá. "I am very much pleased that you have come. Be seated."

The man hung his head and trembled as he sat down. 'Abdu'l-Bahá held his hand and patted his tangled hair.

"Be happy! Be happy!" said 'Abdu'l-Bahá, and told him not to be sad because he was poor. "You can be rich in the Kingdom of God," 'Abdu'l-Bahá told him with a smile.

'Abdu'l-Bahá spoke with him for a long time, and the man realised that he had been wasting his life. He decided he would not beg any more but find work on a farm. When he had saved a little money, he said, then he would grow violets and sell them in the market.

By the time he left 'Abdu'l-Bahá, the man was feeling very happy. He knew that God loved him and wanted him to do something worthwhile with his life.

32

Christmas Dinner

There were many poor people in Haifa and 'Akká, where 'Abdu'l-Bahá lived. In fact, at the time, most people who lived there were poor. But He was sad to see there were also poor people in the rich countries of the West. He was especially sad when He saw rich people in London buying expensive Christmas presents when there were so many people around who did not even have enough bread to eat.

One day He visited a Salvation Army shelter where one thousand poor men had been invited for their Christmas dinner. 'Abdu'l-Bahá told them:

"All the Prophets of God were poor, His Holiness Moses was a mere shepherd.... The poor have ever been humble, and lowly; their hearts are tender.... Christ was poor; Bahá'u'lláh was poor. For forty years He was imprisoned in poverty.... Be ever happy; be not sad! Trust in God."

The men had rarely been spoken to with such love and understanding. Although they were very hungry, some of them forgot to eat while 'Abdu'l-Bahá was speaking.

Before He left, 'Abdu'l-Bahá gave the kind Salvation Army officers money to pay for another good meal for the men at New Year. When they heard this, the men jumped up from their seats and waved their knives and forks in the air and cheered!

33

Fruitful Trees

It was raining as 'Abdu'l-Bahá was being driven through the streets of London. He was on His way to a meeting where nearly sixty mothers and over one hundred children were gathered. Because they were so poor, they were being looked after by a charity.

When 'Abdu'l-Bahá entered the room, He walked among the women and children, beaming with happiness.

"I am very glad to be among you who are blessed in God's name with children," He said. "These little ones will grow to be fruitful trees."

He stopped in front of one of the mothers who was holding a small child who was very pale. 'Abdu'l-Bahá patted the child's head and spoke to her softly. She stretched her tiny hand towards 'Abdu'l-Bahá, and He gently closed it over a bright new shilling.

'Abdu'l-Bahá spoke to every child, even to the youngest baby, and gave them all a silver coin. None of the babies cried and everyone felt loved and peaceful.

"I am truly happy when among the gatherings of the poor," 'Abdu'l-Bahá said afterwards. "It brings full joy to my heart ... for their sufferings draw them nearer to God...."

34

Silver Sixpences

A crowd of children was gathered around 'Abdu'l-Bahá. He was staying with some of the Bahá'ís in a village near London. The children had never before seen anyone who looked like 'Abdu'l-Bahá. He wore a white turban on His head and His long cloak reached down to the ground. He was smiling, and His eyes twinkled when He saw the children.

The younger children gently pulled at 'Abdu'l-Bahá's cloak and held His hands. One by one He lifted them up and gave them a hug. When He put them back on the ground again they found that He had put a little silver sixpence in their hands.

The children ran home to tell their parents about the kind "Holy Man". Before long, whole families began to arrive, wanting to see 'Abdu'l-Bahá. They were all very poor and often hungry. 'Abdu'l-Bahá welcomed them all and gave each one a silver sixpence.

At nine o'clock that evening, a poor man came up the garden path towards the house. He was carrying a baby and his other children were shyly holding onto him.

The lady who owned the house wanted to protect 'Abdu'l-Bahá from seeing any more people that day. She knew He was tired. She also wanted to protect Him from having to give more people money. She told the man that 'Abdu'l-Bahá would not be seeing anyone else that day and said that He was tired and had gone to bed. The man was very disappointed because he had walked six miles to see Him.

The lady meant well, but 'Abdu'l-Bahá did not want to be protected from seeing people! He knew what sad and difficul ives these poor people led. He loved them and wanted to help them. At that moment He came round the corner of the house and saw the poor father with his children. He spoke to them kindly and gave them all a hug.

When the family finally left, they were smiling and happy. Their hearts were full of the love of 'Abdu'l-Bahá – and their hands were full of sixpences!

35

Arab Visitors

When 'Abdu'l-Bahá returned to Haifa after His visits to the West, He was kept very busy. Every day people came to see Him. Sometimes people came who were rich or important. Sometimes they were poor. Once, a group of English people who were on holiday knocked at His door. 'Abdu'l-Bahá welcomed them all.

One day an Arab came to the house. A little while later, another Arab arrived. When they saw each other they became angry because they hated one another. 'Abdu'l-Bahá told them funny stories and they began to laugh. He also told them serious stories and they listened thoughtfully.

"My home is the home of peace," said 'Abdu'l-Bahá. "My home is the home of joy and delight. My home is the home of laughter.... Whoever enters through the portals of this home must go out with gladsome heart."

He told them to embrace one another, and fetched sweets and two silk handkerchiefs to give them.

"Is it not much better to be friends than enemies?" He asked them.

"It seems God directed our steps to your home this morning," they said, as they left the house the best of friends.

36
The Silk Rug

A pilgrim arrived in Haifa with a gift for 'Abdu'l-Bahá. It was a beautiful rug with a pattern of a rose garden on it. It was woven with silver and gold silk thread.

The generous pilgrim asked that the rug be spread at the entrance of the pilgrim house so that 'Abdu'l-Bahá would walk on it when He came in. But when 'Abdu'l-Bahá saw the precious rug on the floor, He said it was far too valuable to be walked upon. There was only one place for such a lovely rug, He said.

Several days later, 'Abdu'l-Bahá and the pilgrims travelled by train to 'Akká. From there, 'Abdu'l-Bahá rode a white donkey for the short distance to Bahjí, where the Shrine of Bahá'u'lláh was. The friends sang as they walked along behind 'Abdu'l-Bahá and His donkey.

When they reached Bahjí, they became quiet. They said prayers, and 'Abdu'l-Bahá reverently placed the beautiful rug in the Shrine of Bahá'u'lláh.

37

The Schoolmaster's Daughters

One of 'Abdu'l-Baháh's friends was a Christian schoolmaster who lived in Haifa. The schoolmaster and his wife had two little girls. They were a happy family but they had a difficult life. The schoolmaster was not paid much for his work and they were very poor. Then his wife became ill and died and he did not know how he was going to look after his daughters. He could not even afford to send them to school.

It was then that a rich friend of 'Abdu'l-Bahá's came from America to Haifa. She wanted to give money to 'Abdu'l-Bahá, either to be used for Himself or for the Faith. He thanked her but said He could not accept it. However, He suggested that she could pay for the schoolmaster's daughters to go to school, and the lady happily agreed to do this.

In those days, many people thought it was not necessary for girls to go to school, but 'Abdu'l-Bahá knew it was very important for girls to be educated. If girls were well educated, then they would be able to teach their own children better, and to help them to love God and to lead good lives.

38

Thieves

A group of Bahá'ís were travelling from Persia to Haifa to visit 'Abdu'l-Bahá. On the way they stayed with the Bahá'ís in Turkey, who gave them some silver pieces to take as a gift for 'Abdu'l-Bahá.

The journey was slow and difficult. However, after three months of travelling, they were nearly at the end of their journey. They arrived in 'Akká, just across the bay from Haifa. But as they were walking through the town, thieves stopped them and threatened them and opened all their cases.

The thieves began to steal everything the Bahá'ís were carrying. They were about to take the bag containing the silver, when one of the Bahá'ís said, "That silver is for 'Abdu'l-Bahá!"

The thieves felt ashamed. They knew 'Abdu'l-Bahá. He had often looked after them when they were poor and cold and hungry.

"'Abdu'l-Bahá fed us. He clothed us, and housed us," they said. And gave back all the silver.

39

Three Shots in the Dark

At one time there was a great deal of trouble in Haifa. Gunmen roamed the streets and killed people and the policemen did not seem to do anything about it. It was a very dangerous time. The Bahá'ís were worried about 'Abdu'l-Bahá because He often went out alone at night to visit poor people.

One night 'Abdu'l-Bahá was returning home after one of these visits. It was late, just past midnight. One of the Bahá'ís followed 'Abdu'l-Bahá at a distance to make sure He was safe.

Suddenly a gun was fired in one of the dark streets nearby. Then a second shot rang out. The Bahá'í who was following 'Abdu'l-Bahá ran towards Him.

There was a flash, and a third shot was heard. The Bahá'í saw two men running away.

But 'Abdu'l-Bahá walked calmly on. He did not panic or stop or even turn His head to see what was happening. He was not at all frightened. He quietly said prayers to Himself and trusted in God to protect Him. He was not going to let any gunmen stop Him from visiting people who needed His help, even if it was dangerous.

40

'Abdu'l-Bahá's Cat

Fugita was a believer who came from Japan. He served in the House of 'Abdu'l-Bahá in Haifa. One of his duties was to look after 'Abdu'l-Bahá's brown cat. He also made 'Abdu'l-Bahá laugh.

At mealtimes, Fugita would sometimes play a game by hiding the cat in the kitchen. But 'Abdu'l-Bahá would always know. He would wait until the end of the meal, then say, "Let the cat out!" and Fugita would jump up with a grin and open the kitchen door.

The cat would be waiting. As soon as the door opened, she would race like a streak of lightning across the room to 'Abdu'l-Bahá. He would laugh and bend down to stroke her. Then He would give her something to eat.

When the cat had eaten her food, she would rub herself against 'Abdu'l-Bahá's feet and purr with happiness!

41

Angel of Carmel

One of the Bahá'ís had many adventures. His name was Hájí Mírzá Haydar Alí. 'Abdu'l-Bahá called him Hájí.

Hájí had travelled to many places telling people about the teachings of Bahá'u'lláh. Once, when he was in Egypt, he was arrested. With other prisoners, he was taken across a desert to a prison.

The prisoners were chained together in pairs. Each one had a foot locked in a wooden block, which made it almost impossible to walk. Hájí explained afterwards how the guards tied each pair of prisoners to a camel by their hands and feet, in such a way that their heads were hanging down. They travelled this way for twelve days, and it was very uncomfortable. But they looked so funny they could not help laughing at each other.

When Hájí grew old, 'Abdu'l-Bahá invited him to live in Haifa so that He could look after him. Hájí spent his time teaching the children to speak Arabic, giving talks to the pilgrims, and writing a book about his adventures.

The Bahá'ís called Hájí "the Angel of Carmel" and loved him very much. Some of them invited him to come to their own countries. But Hájí was now nearly ninety years old and was so weak he often had to stay in bed. 'Abdu'l-Bahá loved him and went to see him every day.

'Abdu'l-Bahá would wrap Hájí in His own cloak and smile and say, "Hájí is ours!" And said that he should stay in Haifa.

42
'Abdu'l-Bahá's Coachman

Isfandiyar was a servant in the House of 'Abdu'l-Bahá. Although he had the same name as the servant who had sometimes looked after 'Abdu'l-Bahá when He was a little boy in Persia, this was someone different. But he was also pure-hearted.

This particular Isfandiyar was busy polishing 'Abdu'l-Bahá's carriage. He then brushed the horses that would pull the carriage until their manes and tails and coats shone like silk. The horses and carriage were now ready to take 'Abdu'l-Bahá to an important ceremony in the town of Haifa.

As Isfandiyar waited in the yard, a car stopped in front of the house. His heart sank. The car had been sent by government officials to take 'Abdu'l-Bahá to the ceremony. Isfandiyar thought he was no longer needed.

But one of the believers came running into the yard. "The Master is asking for you," he said to Isfandiyar. "He is waiting for you to take Him to the ceremony!"

Isfandiyar quickly harnessed the horses to the carriage. Then he led the horses to the front gate. A large, shining black car was parked in the roadway, but 'Abdu'l-Bahá did not take any notice of it. Instead, He climbed into the horse-drawn carriage. Isfandiyar's heart was bursting with joy as he proudly held the reigns and drove 'Abdu'l-Bahá through the streets of Haifa.

They arrived at the house of the Governor of Haifa, where chairs had been set out in the garden and many important people were waiting for 'Abdu'l-Bahá to arrive in the shiny black car.

They were wondering where He had got to, when He quietly walked through a side gate and into the garden.

'Abdu'l-Bahá was given the seat of honour. He had grown fields of lentils and corn and fed thousands of people when there had been a war in the land. Without this food, many people would have died of hunger. The British Government now wanted to thank Him. They were going to make Him a Knight and give Him a medal.

When the ceremony was over, 'Abdu'l-Bahá climbed back into the carriage. He smiled at Isfandiyar and said they could now drive back home!

43

The Sparrow and the Hawk

'Abdu'l-Bahá was walking in His garden one morning when a large hawk flew overhead. It was looking for a small bird to eat for its dinner.

The hawk hovered over the garden. It had seen a small sparrow down below. The sparrow was frightened when it saw the black shadow overhead. It knew the hawk was about to swoop down to kill it. Its tiny heart began to beat faster and faster. In panic, it looked around for somewhere safe to hide and flew straight towards 'Abdu'l-Bahá, as though it knew He would protect it.

The hawk gave up and flew away. It decided to look somewhere else for its dinner!

44

The Garden

'Abdu'l-Bahá made a beautiful garden round the Shrine where Bahá'u'lláh was buried. Twice a year He carried at least one hundred flower pots from the Ridván Garden outside of 'Akká to the Shrine in Bahjí. All the pilgrims and the Bahá'ís living in 'Akká helped. They made a procession, walking two by two. Each person carried a flower pot on his or her shoulder and chanted prayers and sang as they travelled along.

'Abdu'l-Bahá worked hard in the garden. He was now quite old, but He stood for hours pumping water from a well and then carrying it in jars to pour onto the flowers. Sometimes He made sixty trips to fetch enough water and often became ill with a fever.

The Bahá'ís begged Him not to work so hard and to let them carry the jars of water instead. To please the friends, 'Abdu'l-Bahá reluctantly agreed. But He became very unhappy. He wanted so much to do something special for Bahá'u'lláh. He loved working in the garden and making it beautiful.

Two weeks passed by. Then 'Abdu'l-Bahá called the friends together. He told them that He had done as they wished and not worked in the garden. He asked them to please allow Him to work there again.

The friends felt terrible. They thought they had been helping 'Abdu'l-Bahá. But all they had done was to make Him unhappy. Never again did they try to stop Him from working in the garden round the Shrine of Bahá'u'lláh.

45

The Passing of 'Abdu'l-Bahá

One month before 'Abdu'l-Bahá died, He was talking to a guest called Dr Bey. The doctor had just received a telegram to say that his brother had died.

"Sorry not," 'Abdu'l-Bahá told Dr Bey, "for he is only transferred from this plane to a higher one." Then 'Abdu'l-Bahá whispered to Dr Bey, "I too shall soon be transferred, for my days are numbered."

'Abdu'l-Bahá gently patted the doctor on the shoulder, and added, "And it will be in the days that are shortly to come."

Although He was now very tired, 'Abdu'l-Bahá continued to give His loving attention to everyone. He held meetings in His room, and blessed the marriage of two of the believers. The mayor of Haifa and other officials came to see Him and ask for His advice.

Some of the Báhá'ís had been to a gathering on Mount Carmel and were sad that 'Abdu'l-Bahá had not been able to be with them.

"The friends must not attach any importance to the absence of my body," said 'Abdu'l-Bahá. "In spirit I am, and shall always be, with the friends."

He asked if everyone was well. When He was told that they were, He said, "Very good, very good!"

He told His sister not to be sad. "For a long time I desired to join my Father, the Blessed Beauty [Bahá'u'lláh]," 'Abdu'l-Bahá told her, "and now my prayer is granted, how happy, how joyous, how rested I am. Therefore, grieve not."

That night 'Abdu'l-Bahá died, and His soul passed happily from this world to the next.

46

'Abdu'l-Bahá's Funeral

'Abdu'l-Bahá's sister made all the arrangements for the funeral. And there had never been such a funeral in the Holy Land before. Ten thousand people came – the High Commissioner of the land, the chief officials of the Government, and Jews, Christians, Muslims, Druze, Egyptians, Persians, Greeks, Turks, Kurds, Americans, Europeans, Palestinians, the rich, the poor, men, women and children! Near the front of the procession was a group of Muslim and Christian Boy Scouts marching together. They held a banner above their heads and slowly walked along, followed by a choir chanting the Words of God.

It took two hours for the funeral procession to make its way up Mount Carmel. Here, 'Abdu'l-Bahá's coffin was laid in a room in the Shrine of the Báb.

"O great revered Sleeper!" cried one of the Christians. "Thou hast been good to us, thou hast guided us, thou hast taught us.... Thou hast shown loving-kindness to the people...."

Every day, poor people came to His house and were fed. And a week later, corn was given in the name of 'Abdu'l-Bahá to a thousand poor people in Haifa. Then, forty days after the funeral, 'Abdu'l-Bahá's family held a feast in His memory. Long tables were laden with food and decorated with purple bougainvillea and white narcissus and large dishes of golden oranges from 'Abdu'l-Bahá's garden. Hundreds of people were invited from different religions and different countries. 'Abdu'l-Bahá had loved them all. He was the "Servant of Bahá'u'lláh", the "Centre of the Covenant", a "shelter for all mankind". And He was an example for all of us to follow.

"I am the servant of the Blessed Perfection
[Bahá'u'lláh]. In Baghdád I was a child.
Then and there He announced to me the Word,
and I believed in Him.
As soon as He proclaimed to me the Word,
I threw myself at His Holy Feet...."
'Abdu'l-Bahá

Bibliography

'Abdu'l-Bahá, *The Promulgation of Universal Peace* (Wilmette: Bahá'í Publishing Trust, 1982)

'Abdu'l-Bahá, *Selections from the Writings of 'Abdu'l-Bahá*, (Haifa: Bahá'í World Centre, 1978)

Bahá'í Prayers (Wilmette: Bahá'í Publishing Trust, 2002)

Balyuzi, H. M., *'Abdu'l-Bahá, The Centre of the Covenant of Bahá'u'lláh* (Oxford: George Ronald, 1959)

Balyuzi, H. M., *Bahá'u'lláh, The King of Glory* (Oxford: George Ronald, 1980)

Blomfield, Lady, *The Chosen Highway* (Wilmette: Bahá'í Publishing Trust, 1940)

Chase, Thornton, *In Galilee* (Los Angeles: Kalimát Press, 1985)

Cobb, Stanley, *Memories of 'Abdu'l-Bahá*, published *In His Presence – Visits to 'Abdu'l-Bahá* (Los Angeles: Kalimát Press, 1989)

Esslemont, J. E., *Bahá'u'lláh and the New Era* (Wilmette: Bahá'í Publishing Trust, 1980)

Gail, Marzieh, *The Sheltering Branch* (Oxford: George Ronald, 1959)

Goodall, Helen S., and Goodall Cooper, Ella, *Daily Lessons Received at 'Akká, January 1908* (Wilmette: Bahá'í Publishing Trust, 1979)

Haydar-'Alí, Hájí Mírzá, *Stories from the Delight of Hearts – Memoirs of Hájí Mírzá Haydar-'Alí*, translated by A. Q. Faizi (Los Angeles: Kalimát Press, 1980)

Honnold, Annamarie, *Vignettes from the Life of 'Abdu'l-Bahá* (Oxford: George Ronald, 1982)

Ives, Colby, *Portals to Freedom* (Northampton: George Ronald, 1943) (note: now Oxford not Northampton)

Lakshman-Lepain, Rajwantee, *The Life of Thomas Breakwell* (London: Bahá'í Publishing Trust, 1998)

Maxwell, May, *An Early Pilgrimage* (Oxford: George Ronald, 1969)

Phelps, Myron, *The Master in 'Akká* (Los Angeles: Kalimát Press, 1985)

Rabbání, Rúhíyyih, *The Priceless Pearl* (London: Bahá'í Publishing Trust, 1969)

Rutstein, Nathan, *He Loved and Served – The Story of Curtis Kelsey* (Oxford: George Ronald, 1982)

Shoghi Effendi, *God Passes By* (Wilmette: Bahá'í Publishing Trust, 1957)

Shoghi Effendi with Sitarih Khanum (Lady Blomfield), *The Passing of 'Abdu'l-Bahá*, (London: Bahá'í Publishing Trust, 1922)

Shoghi Effendi, *World Order of Bahá'u'lláh* (Wilmette: Bahá'í Publishing Trust, 1978)

Star of the West, vols. 2, 5 and 8 (Oxford: George Ronald, 1978)

Taherzadeh, Adib, *The Revelation of Bahá'u'lláh, Ba<u>gh</u>dád 1853–63*, vol. 1 (Oxford: George Ronald, 1974)

Thompson, Juliet, *The Diary of Juliet Thompson*, (Los Angeles: Kalimát Press, 1983)

Ward, Allan L., *239 Days – 'Abdu'l-Bahá's Journey in America* (Wilmette: Bahá'í Publishing Trust, 1979)

33 "Fruitful Trees": *Star of the West*, (vol. 2 in GR reprint) vol. III, no. 18, February 7, 1913, pp. 9–10

34 "Silver Sixpences": Honnold, *Vignettes from the Life of 'Abdu'l-Bahá*, pp. 62–63

35 "Arab Visitors": Balyuzi, *'Abdu'l-Bahá, The Centre of the Covenant*, p. 405; *Star of the West*, (vol. 5 in GR reprint) vol. IX, no. 3, April 28, 1918, pp. 39–40

36 "The Silk Rug": Honnold, *Vignettes from the Life of 'Abdu'l-Bahá*, pp. 59–60; Balyuzi, *'Abdu'l-Bahá, The Centre of the Covenant*, pp. 516–517

37 "The Schoolmaster's Daughters": Phelps, *The Master in 'Akká*, pp. 139–140

38 "Thieves": Honnold, *Vignettes from the Life of 'Abdu'l-Bahá*, p. 163

39 "Three Shots in the Dark": Honnold, *Vignettes from the Life of 'Abdu'l-Bahá*, pp. 134–135

40 "'Abdu'l-Bahá's Cat": Rutstein, *He Loved and Served*, pp. 73–74

41 "Angel of Carmel": Haydar-'Ali, *The Delight of Hearts*, pp. 46, 47, 162

42 "'Abdu'l-Bahá's Coachman": Honnold, *Vignettes from the Life of 'Abdu'l-Bahá*, p. 17; Blomfield, *The Chosen Highway*, pp. 214–215

43 "The Sparrow and the Hawk": Goodall and Cooper, *Daily Lessons Received at 'Akká, January 1908*, p. 64

44 "The Garden": Balyuzi, *'Abdu'l-Bahá, The Centre of the Covenant*, pp. 131–132

45 "The Passing of 'Abdu'l-Baha": Shoghi Effendi, *God Passes By*, pp. 311–314; *The Passing of 'Abdu'l-Bahá* (booklet by Shoghi Effendi and Lady Blomfield)

46 'Abdu'l-Bahá's Funeral": Shoghi Effendi, *God Passes By*, pp. 311–314; *The Passing of 'Abdu'l-Bahá* (booklet by Shoghi Effendi and Lady Blomfield)

Quotation at end: *Bahá'u'lláh and the New Era*, p. 52. See *Star of the West*, (vol. 5 in GR reprint) vol. IX, no. 18, February 7, 1919, p. 203 for a slightly different version of this quotation, and *God Passes By*, p. 241, for mention of it.

The Purest Branch: Mirzá Mihdí

Contents

1

The Land of Light

This story began in Núr, the Land of Light, in the north of Persia. You could smell the scent of white-blossomed trees and hear rivers of running water. There were ferns and forests, flowers and waterfalls, and valleys red with pomegranates. Stories were told of an invisible volcano that bubbled away in the heart of a mountain, and a cool, scented breeze that blew up from a well so deep that a bucket and rope never reached the water. Bird-song hovered on the air and mingled with the sound of children laughing.

The youngest child was called Mihdí and his eyes were full of kindness. His fragile face was flushed with joy and his manner very gentle. His mother, Navváb, quietly called his name and he ran into the house with his sister and brother.

2

The House in Tihrán

When the long, hot days of summer ended, Mihdí and his Family left their peaceful house in the country and returned to live in their house in Tihrán, the capital city of Persia.

One day, Mihdí's Father, Bahá'u'lláh, was arrested and unjustly put into prison! A crowd of people clashing cymbals and shouting attacked the house, throwing stones and breaking the doors and windows!

As elegant vases crashed to the ground, Navváb gathered up her children. They ran out of the house, holding onto their mother. Then they quickly walked through the lanes, taking care not to be seen, until they came to a part of the town where nobody knew them.

A kind relative helped them to rent two rooms in a house where they could hide in safety.

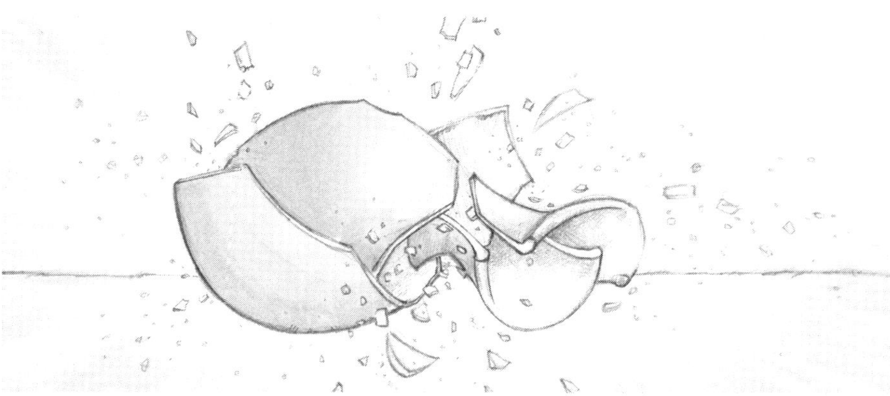

3

Hiding

Every day Navváb went to the house of her sister to find out if she had any news of Bahá'u'lláh in prison. The prison was a black pit, called the Siyáh Chál, and was under the ground without any light or windows. Navváb usually took 'Abdu'l-Bahá, her eight-year-old son, with her. Bahíyyih, who was six, stayed behind to look after Mihdí, her little brother. Bahíyyih was sensible and kind, and Mihdí tried to be brave as he looked into her eyes, which were a soft bluey-grey like their mother's. Bahíyyih hugged him tight and they sat very still when they heard people outside shouting.

4

The Wonderful Message

Every day Navváb and the children prayed that Bahá'u'lláh would be set free. And at last, four months later, He was allowed to come home to His Family.

Bahá'u'lláh slowly came out of the black pit and into the brilliant sunshine. He was thin and ill with deep sores on His neck where chains had been hung as He lay in the dark. But a light seemed to shine from Bahá'u'lláh and His face was bright with happiness. While He was chained in the underground cell, God had given Him a wonderful Message. He had told Him the knowledge of everything that has ever been, and teachings to bring peace to the world.

"This thing is not from Me," said Bahá'u'lláh later, "but from One Who is Almighty and All-Knowing."

5

Banished from Persia

Although everyone was very happy that Bahá'u'lláh was free, there was another worry. When Bahá'u'lláh left the prison, the government said He was not allowed to stay in Persia. He had to go away to live in another country. He was given just one month to get ready to leave.

The Family did not have any money as it had all been stolen. They did not even have any warm clothes to wear as everything had been left behind when they escaped from their house. Navváb had to sell her jewellery and some of her clothes to pay for food for the journey.

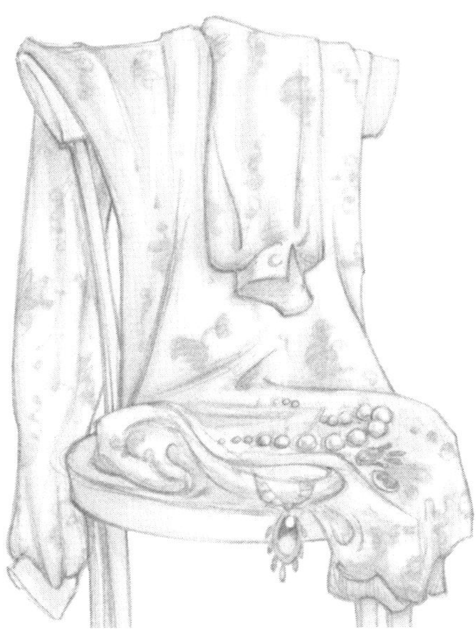

6

Left Behind

One cold, winter's morning, Mihdí awoke to the sound of people packing. The Family's few belongings were tied together and his mother and sister climbed into a howdah, a small wooden carriage tied onto a mule. 'Abdu'l-Bahá also got ready, and Bahá'u'lláh was helped onto a horse, although He was still feeling poorly. Mihdí tried not to cry when his mother told him that because he was not very strong he could not go with them. His parents thought he would become ill and die if he went on such a long journey through mountains in the middle of winter. Feeling very sad, Navváb had to leave him behind in Tihrán with her mother. Mihdí waved goodbye to his Father and mother and sister and brother. He did not know when he would see them again.

7

Patiently Waiting

Mihdí was four years old when he was left behind in Persia. Nobody knows what he did all the years as he patiently waited. But we can guess that he played with his cousins, was taught to read and do beautiful writing. Perhaps he knew some prayers by heart and said them when he was lonely.

Year after year passed by, and still he patiently waited. For a long time he had been strong enough to make the journey, but there had never been anyone who could take him. Then, when he was eleven, a relative decided to go to Ba<u>gh</u>dád and agreed to take Mihdí with her.

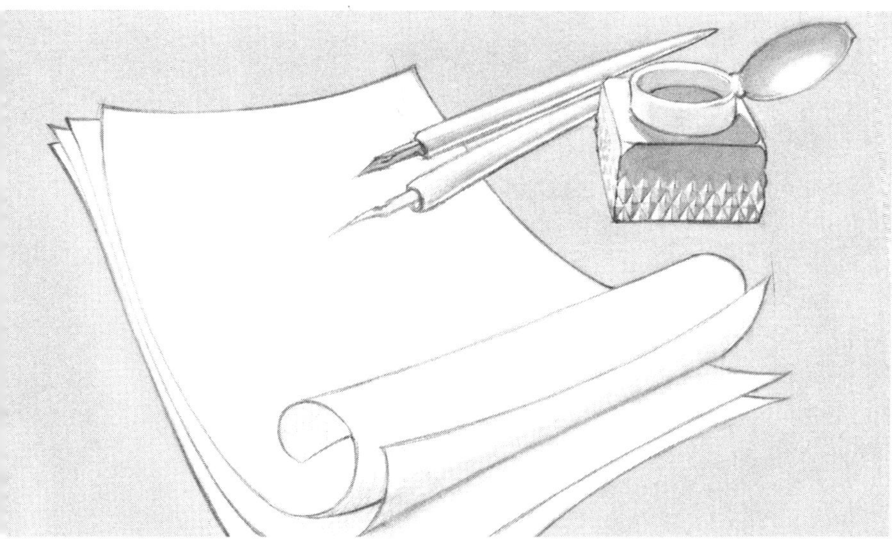

8

Tihrán to Baghdád

Mihdí probably did not travel in the middle of winter through snow like his parents and brother and sister, but left when the weather was warmer. He may even have gone an easier way which didn't go through the mountains. But it was still very dangerous to travel the lonely route to Iráq from the north of Persia. Bandits were known to attack travellers and rob them of all their money. And there were still tigers living in the mountains which might attack if they were hungry.

He would have passed by tumbled down houses where owls now lived. Passed isolated farmhouses sleeping in the sun. Passed barefoot children playing in the fields. Passed shepherd boys with their flocks of sheep. There were bound to be other travellers on the road, and perhaps they called out "Peace be with you!" and asked Mihdí where he was going.

As he rode along, seeing nothing but sunburnt land that seemed to go on for ever, Mihdí must have wondered when he would come to the end of his journey. Then, one day, he caught a glimpse of the walls of Baghdád in the distance.

9

Together Again

When Mihdí arrived in Baghdád, he was welcomed with great rejoicing. He could see the love in his mother's eyes and the smiles of his brother and sister. And when he entered the presence of Bahá'u'lláh, he must have felt he was now in heaven. Every bird seemed to sing more beautifully. Every smile was filled with love. He sat at the feet of Bahá'u'lláh and heard the wonderful words of God. Love and peace, joy and happiness flooded over his heart and soul. Like a flower that had waited a long, long time for water, he drank and drank of the love of God, and his soul grew and grew.

10

Baghdád

Life became exciting for Mihdí in Baghdád. All day people came to the house. Princes. Poor men. Enemies. Friends. Bahá'u'lláh greeted them all with love and all of them left feeling happy.

Bahá'u'lláh walked through the streets of Baghdád, greeting people and visiting their houses. One of the believers was a carpenter; another, a shepherd; a third, a baker of bread. Mihdí's sister, Bahíyyih, helped her mother to look after the many guests who came to the house. His brother, 'Abdu'l-Bahá, was busy writing explanations of the teachings of God and talking to learned men in the mosques. And Mihdí's uncle Kalím used to wash the clothes and cook when everyone else was busy.

Mihdí also found ways to make himself useful. He was humble and gentle and thoughtful and kind, and the believers loved him dearly.

11

The River Tigris

Mihdí noticed that one of the friends, even though he was rich and well-educated, used to go to Bahá'u'lláh's house each night and sweep the road outside. He would then collect the dust in his cloak, carry it carefully down to the river, and throw it into the water. When someone asked why he did this, he replied that the dust had been made holy because Bahá'u'lláh had walked on it, and he did not think it was right for anyone else to walk on it afterwards.The name of the river was the Tigris, and Bahá'u'lláh often walked along its banks, revealing the Words of God. Mihdí also walked by this river, and a wonderful thing was about to happen in a garden on the other side.

12

Across the River

Three years after Mihdí arrived in Baghdád, the members of the Holy Family were suddenly ordered to leave. They were being sent away to another town in the north of the country. The government officials in Persia were worried because so many people were visiting Bahá'u'lláh and they wanted Him to be sent further away from the border of their country. At first, Bahá'u'lláh said He would go alone, but His Family and friends wanted to go with Him.

While their belongings were being packed for the journey, Bahá'u'lláh decided to go to a garden on the other side of the river Tigris so that people could visit Him and say goodbye. As He walked down the path towards the river, people crowded round Him, begging Him not to leave. But Bahá'u'lláh knew that whatever happened, it was part of the Will of God. He moved slowly along the path, stopping to speak to people and comfort them with words of love. When He reached the river, He stepped into a small boat. Mihdí was one of those who went with Him. They were then rowed across the river to a lovely rose-filled garden.

13

The Garden of Paradise

As Mihdí arrived in the garden, a prayer was being chanted from a nearby mosque. The words "God is Most Great" filled the sky and all of the garden. There were flowers everywhere and, at night, the sound of nightingales singing.

Tents were put up beneath the trees and day after day people came to visit Bahá'u'lláh. When the governor of Baghdád came, he humbly bowed before Him. He asked Bahá'u'lláh if there was anything he could do to help Him. Bahá'u'lláh asked the governor to be kind to the believers. The governor promised he would.

During these days, which are called the Twelve Days of Ridván, something very important happened. Bahá'u'lláh said He was the Manifestation of God the whole of the world was waiting for.

As Bahá'u'lláh chanted the Words of God, the trees seemed to bow as He passed beneath them. The air was full of the perfume of roses, and the tiniest flowers reached up to kiss the passing hem of His robe.

14

Another Journey

When the twelve days ended, the tents were folded up and the Holy Family had to leave the Garden of Paradise. The people of Ba*gh*dád did not want them to go. Some of them cried. And some of them tried to stop Bahá'u'lláh from leaving by throwing themselves in front of His horse, while others held onto His horse's stirrups.

The Holy Family travelled for many miles along a path beside the river Tigris. Ten friendly soldiers went with them to protect them on the way. These soldiers had been told by the governor of Ba*gh*dád to treat Bahá'u'lláh and His Family with the greatest love and respect.

When they came near to a village or town, the soldiers would beat on drums to let the inhabitants know that someone important was coming. As Bahá'u'llah passed by, the people would come out of their houses to greet Him.

The journey took more than a hundred days, through woods and valleys and mountains. At night, tents were put up on the banks of the river. Horses were groomed and food was cooked and everyone was busy. After riding all day in the sun, 'Abdu'l-Bahá would sometimes swim in the river, which was cold from icy water flowing down from the snow-topped mountains. Mihdí and the other young boys no doubt went swimming too.

15

Adventures

Mihdí saw many new things on this journey. At one time they passed close by the mountain where Noah's Ark was said to have landed after the flood went down. At another time they came to a village where all the houses were built under the ground. The people said it made the houses warmer to build them that way.

The travellers and their animals often had to squeeze through narrow mountain passes. It took four men to push the heavily laden donkeys and mules through to the other side. Bahá'u'lláh often rode His horse, but sometimes He travelled in one of the howdahs.

One day, Bahá'u'lláh was travelling in a howdah along a narrow ledge on the side of a mountain. On one side was rock reaching up to the sky, and on the other, a long drop down to the ground below. A man was holding the bridle of the mule carrying the howdah with Bahá'u'lláh inside, guiding it carefully along the ledge. For a second, the man let go, and the mule began to slip towards the edge. With everyone else, Mihdí watched in horror. The mule desperately tried to find its footing on the loose stones. Finally, it managed to stop. A little bit further and it would have fallen over the edge. Bahá'u'lláh was safe! Everyone sighed in relief. A large bottle of perfume broke, and the air became full of the scent of roses.

16

Walking Through the Night

At the end of each day, everyone was exhausted and fell asleep as soon as they had eaten. But the two friends responsible for the cooking could not go to sleep immediately. They had to work for several hours more, washing the pots and pans and dishes.

Spring had now turned to summer and the weather was very hot. Instead of travelling through the day, they often travelled in the middle of the night when it was cooler. This seemed a good idea, but by the time the cooks had finished their work it was almost time to set off again and they often did not get enough sleep. And one day something comical happened. As they were walking along, the cooks fell asleep. But they continued to walk with their eyes shut. Every now and then they would dream they had come to a small stream and jump over it, but there was never anything there! They looked so funny leaping all over the place that everyone was laughing.

It was a dark and windy night when one of these cooks got lost. He lay down to sleep for a few minutes but did not wake up until five hours later. By then, everyone had disappeared. He was lost for hours. In the dark, no-one noticed at first that he was missing. He finally caught up with the others when they stopped to set up camp the next morning. The first person he met was Mihdí's uncle Kalim, who told him that some of the friends were just about to look for him.

17

Finding Food

Everyone had an important job to do on the journey. Every day, Mihdí would see 'Abdu'l-Bahá riding on ahead hoping to buy food from the farmers. More than seventy people needed to be fed, as well as thirty-six animals. But there was a famine in the land and some days it was impossible to buy anything. One time, 'Abdu'l-Bahá went up to a farmer who was cutting a field of straw and politely asked if He could buy some. The farmer said, "Open your sack." But when 'Abdu'l-Bahá held open an empty sack, the man just put a few handfuls of straw into it and refused to give Him any more.

But other people were more generous. In a town called Khárpút, the chief leader of the town gave them ten cart loads of rice, ten sacks of barley, ten sheep, bags of sugar, pounds of butter, and cherries! They stayed in Khárpút for a week and everyone, including Mihdí, had a good rest. 'Abdu'l-Bahá was so tired He slept for two days and two nights.

18

The Barber

It was in the town of Khárpút that something else happened. It had to do with a believer called Ustád, who was Bahá'u'lláh's barber. Ustád had never gone to school and could not read or write, but he was very clever and understood the important things in life. He used to compose beautiful poetry about Bahá'u'lláh. As Ustád recited his poems, one of the friends would write them down.

Mihdí's uncles always came to Ustád to have their hair cut or their beards trimmed. There were good and faithful uncles, like Uncle Kalím and Uncle Qúlí. But there was also one bad uncle who was jealous of Bahá'u'lláh and caused a lot of trouble. This bad uncle would tell Ustád and the other friends not to listen to what Bahá'u'lláh said, but to listen to him instead.

Ustád the barber took no notice of what the jealous uncle said. Whenever this uncle told Ustád to do something that he was not sure was right, he would go straight away to Bahá'u'lláh and ask what he should do.

On this particular day, the bad uncle and his young son went to the public bath where Ustád was working. The uncle ordered Ustád: "Shave my boy's head!" Ustád did not think this was a good idea. It was not the custom for children to have their heads shaved. He decided to ask Bahá'u'lláh whether he should do this or not. Bahá'u'lláh told him not to do it. When Ustád refused to shave the boy's head, the uncle was furious. Ustád tried not to take any notice and continued to do his work, but inside he was very upset.

While all this was happening, Mihdí came into the public bath. All the friends loved him and enjoyed being with him. Although Mihdí was still a young boy, Ustád respected him because he was always polite and humble. Ustád's sadness immediately vanished when Mihdí came into the room. When he was telling this story afterwards, Ustád said he felt so happy and calm when he saw Mihdí, he forgot about everything else, including the troublesome uncle!

19
Son of Abraham

Bahá'u'lláh and His followers came one day to a wild and beautiful place called Irbil, where the Kurdish people lived. On one side was a river, and on the other side a castle built on top of a mountain. Many of the Kurds were nomads and travelled from place to place, wandering over the borders between one country and another, but for special occasions they gathered together in Irbil to celebrate.

As Mihdí rode into the town, he saw there was a grand festival taking place. There were crowds of people dressed in their best clothes. The men had colourful scarves wound round their heads, like turbans, and wore baggy trousers that were narrow at the ankle. Those who were rich wore long, finely embroidered waist-coats. They were very handsome, although some of them looked rather fierce and had daggers glinting in the sashes tied round their waists.

The mouth-watering smell of herbs and fragrant rice filled the air, and the nomad's children were hovering hungrily around pots of food their mothers were cooking. This was an important holy day when everyone remembered a story about the Prophet Abraham and one of His sons. Three thousand years before, Abraham had offered to give His son as a sacrifice to God. Abraham was about to do this when God sent an angel telling Him to stop. But because Abraham had wanted to give God the most precious gift He could think of, God was very pleased with Him and blessed Him and His Family for ever.

At first, the friends were frightened when they saw the fierce Kurds. In another town, some Kurds had thrown stones at them and refused to sell them food. But when Bahá'u'lláh rode into Irbil with His son Mihdí and the rest of the believers, He was greeted with great respect. Some of these Kurds had met Bahá'u'lláh before, when He had spent two years praying to God in the mountains. Their leader came forward with plates full of food to welcome Him.

20

Constantinople

The travellers arrived in the busy town of Constantinople. There was a large and colourful market here which sold everything from parrots to gold earrings. Beautiful mosques gleamed in the sun, and the streets were buzzing with people. Merchants arrived every day from distant lands with goods piled high on their yellow camels. Others came by boat on the Bosphorus Sea that flowed through the city.

Mihdí and his family were just getting settled and getting to know people, when, four months later, they were ordered to move off again. This time, they had to go even further north, to a town called Adrianople. They repacked their belongings and travelled another twelve days over stony roads and bumpy bridges. By this time, it was winter again, and so cold that the rivers froze. They had to break the ice and melt it every time they needed a drink of water.

21

Adrianople

Adrianople was a town near the border of the country. During the five years Bahá'u'lláh was there, Bahá'ís came from hundreds of miles to see Him, and many of them stayed. They often gave up everything they owned to make the journey.

A few of these friends lived in a house close to the one where Mihdí was living with his Family, and he noticed how loving they were to one another. Each day, one of these friends stayed at home to do the housework, look after the garden, go to the market to buy the food, cook the meals and do the washing. When he had washed the dishes after the last meal had been eaten at night, one of the others took over the duties.

Whoever was doing the housework for the day never felt cross or resentful. Each one acted as though he was the host and did everything he could to make the others feel comfortable and happy.

In the evenings, they had happy meetings together, and sometimes Bahá'u'lláh visited them. Mihdí, too, visited these friends and shared in their love and happiness.

22

Writing the Words of God

As everyone settled down to live in Adrianople, many of the friends worked by making things and opening shops. One person made clothes, another baked bread, another sold herbs for medicine.

Because they had given up everything to be with Bahá'u'lláh, they never had much money and their houses were very simple. No silver ornaments stood on the shelves. No expensive paintings hung on the walls. No silken rugs were laid on the floor. Often, there were not even beds, or tables, or chairs. And sometimes they had nothing to eat or drink except water and a handful of dates. But nobody minded. When Bahá'u'lláh was with them, the whitewashed walls and bare, stone floors seemed like a palace to everyone gathered there. Bahá'u'lláh would laugh and drink tea and chant wonderful prayers in their company.

While Bahá'u'lláh was in Adrianople, He wrote to the kings and rulers of the world, telling them how to bring peace to their countries. And He often asked Mihdí to write down the Words as they came like a rush of pure, sparkling water, so fast that Mihdí had difficulty writing them. The pen Mihdí used was a hollow reed, and it sang a high note as it covered the pages.

Then Mihdí would quietly go away on his own to write everything out in his beautiful writing.

23

The Man Who Pretended

People said that Mihdí was very much like 'Abdu'l-Bahá, his older brother. They were both kind and tender-hearted. They were often present when guests came to visit Bahá'u'lláh. Most of these visitors were sincere and wonderful believers. But occasionally one arrived who was not so good. Mihdí was with his Father one day when one of the not-so-good visitors came.

The visitor had been travelling around Persia giving talks, and because so many people had flattered him and said how clever he was, he had become proud and conceited. He thought he was better than everyone else.

When this man asked to meet Bahá'u'lláh, he only pretended to be meek and humble. He knew that Bahá'u'lláh's knowledge came from God, whereas his knowledge only came from books. He knew Bahá'u'lláh was a greater person than he was, but it seems the thought did not please him. Although Bahá'u'lláh knew the man was not sincere, He did not turn him away but kindly agreed to see him.

The man arrived at the house and was taken up the stairs to a room where Bahá'u'lláh and Mihdí were waiting to welcome him. As soon as the man saw Bahá'u'lláh, he began to make himself tremble all over. He fell to the ground, pretending he had fainted because of the greatness and majesty of Bahá'u'lláh.

The man was big and heavy, but Mihdí immediately ran forward to try to lift him up. However, Bahá'u'lláh knew the man had not really fainted. He quietly told Mihdí to leave him alone, saying that the man would be able to get up by himself. Sure enough, the man soon stood up without needing help from anyone.

Many visitors who came to see Bahá'u'lláh really did faint, but they were not pretending like the man who was insincere. When these other visitors fainted, they were lovingly helped to their feet and looked after until they felt better.

24

Sweets

Mihdí woke up one morning to find the house surrounded by soldiers. No-one was allowed in or out. When 'Abdu'l-Bahá enquired what was happening, He was told that an order had come for Bahá'u'lláh to leave Adrianople. At first, the authorities said that the Bahá'ís would all be separated, but in the end they agreed that most of them could stay together. They were being sent to the prison city of 'Akká.

They were not given any time to prepare for their journey by sea to 'Akká. Some of the friends managed to give them a few loaves of bread and a little cheese, but it was not nearly enough for so many people and there was no food to buy on the boat.

Four days later, they reached the port of Alexandria, where they had to change ships to continue their journey. They were sailing out of the harbour when the ship suddenly stopped. People leant over the sides, wondering what was happening. The captain had noticed a small boat being rowed towards them. On the boat was a young man holding two letters addressed to Bahá'u'lláh. One of the letters was from Nabíl-i-Azam, a believer who was imprisoned in the city. The other letter was from a new believer, a doctor called Fáris who was imprisoned with him. Nabíl was sending his love to Bahá'u'lláh. Fáris was asking to be accepted as a true Bahá'í.

Bahá'ú'lláh was standing on the deck with the friends when He received the letters. He read them out loud and everyone was very happy. While the captain waited to set sail again, Bahá'u'lláh revealed a Tablet for Fáris and Nabíl, telling them that soon they would be released from prison. 'Abdu'l-Bahá also wrote a letter. And Mihdí sent a gift of some almond sweets for the two believers.

When the young man returned to Nabíl and Fáris in prison, he shouted out loud, "I have seen the face of the Heavenly Father!" And Fáris kissed his eyes for they had seen the face of Bahá'u'lláh.

In part of his letter, Fáris had written:

"O thou the desolate city of 'Akká! Thou art clapping thy hands in fervent joy ... for the Lord in His great glory will bless thy land with His footsteps."

25

The Most Great Prison

"They are coming, Lord! They are coming!"

The seagulls circled round the sky, shouting the news above the Most Great Prison. The people stood upon the city walls, straining their eyes to try to see Bahá'u'lláh and the believers being brought by boat across the bay to 'Akká.

Mihdí stood on the deck beneath the scorching sun. It was August and very hot and no wind blew. The whole journey from Adrianople had been uncomfortable. The first two boats had been so crowded it had been impossible for anyone to lie down to rest. As well as Bahá'u'lláh and the Bahá'ís, there had been many other passengers on board. Some of these other passengers had not washed for days, maybe weeks, and were very smelly. It had made the journey unpleasant for everyone. When the Holy Family and the friends had arrived in Haifa, they were put on another boat to sail across the bay to 'Akka, on the final part of their journey. And this was the worse part. There was no shelter on deck from the burning sun. And, to make matters worse, there was hardly any wind to fill the sails and blow the boat across the water. Very slowly, it drifted towards the Most Great Prison.

It took eight hours to cross the small stretch of water. As they drew nearer to the strong walls surrounding the city, Mihdí saw crowds of people waving their fists and shouting at them. The people of the town had been told lies about the believers and thought they were murderers and thieves! They did not know that the Bahá'ís had not done anything wrong.

The prisoners were ordered to leave the boat and walk through the shallow water to the shore. Mihdí waded ashore among the others.

With wet clothes clinging round his legs, Mihdí found himself being led with Bahá'u'lláh and nearly seventy believers along the narrow streets and up a flight of steps and through a gate into the prison. Then the gate slammed shut behind them.

26

The Pilgrim Who Could Not See

At first the friends fell very ill when they entered the Most Great Prison. The water was bad, and the bread was black and so full of salt that nobody could eat it. Mothers had no milk to give to their babies and children cried with hunger. Mihdí saw two brothers die, their arms around each other. But the guards soon came to love and trust the Bahá'ís. They saw how gentle and kind they were and how they helped each other. And when 'Abdu'l-Bahá asked for some of the believers to be allowed to go to the market to buy fresh bread, the guards agreed, so long as a guard went with them.

Pilgrims began to arrive in 'Akká, having walked hundreds of miles to get there. But when they arrived, they were not allowed to enter the prison. Some of them got as far as the wall that surrounded the town, and there they stood, hour after hour, hoping at least to see Bahá'u'lláh waving. When they caught a glimpse of His face or the wave of His hand through the bars of the prison window, they would return the hundreds of miles to their homes with hearts full of love and happiness.

One of the people who came was Nabíl, the believer who, with Fáris, had sent Bahá'u'lláh a letter from prison. He disguised himself so the soldiers would not know he was a Bahá'í, but enemies of the Faith soon recognised him and he was ordered to leave 'Akká without seeing Bahá'u'lláh. He wandered about the countryside for nine months, hoping for the chance to come again into the city.

One day the Family noticed an elderly man standing all day on the outer wall, staring towards the prison. He was the uncle of Bahá'u'lláh's cook. But his eyesight was poor and he could not see when Bahá'u'lláh waved His hand through the window. Eventually, the man sadly turned away and went to live in a cave in the mountains.The Holy Family were in tears because they felt so sorry for the nearly blind believer. And Bahá'u'lláh said that something would happen soon that would make it possible for the Bahá'ís to come and see Him.

27

Mihdí's Fall

It was late on a summer's afternoon and Bahá'u'lláh was resting. He told Mihdí that He did not need his help any more that day, so His son climbed the steep steps to the rooftop. Here, the wind was cool and the sky so near it seemed he could reach up with his hand and touch it. His eyes rested a while on the blue, lapping sea and the long hazy line of Mount Carmel. Away to the north were flower-filled fields and the distant high peak of Mount Hermon.

He shut his eyes as he walked up and down, and the sky became full of his chanting. The poem he sang was one Bahá'u'lláh had revealed when He was alone with God in the mountains. It was praising the Holy Spirit of God that had filled His Soul in the dungeon.

Mihdí was so full of joy he forgot where he was and fell through an open skylight. He fell through the air and landed with a crash on a sharp wooden crate beneath him. The friends ran to his aid and carried him gently to lie in his cell. He lovingly smiled and thanked them.

28

The Sacrifice

When Bahá'u'lláh heard the crash as Mihdí fell through the roof onto the floor of the prison, He came out of His room to ask him what had happened. Mihdí explained that he had always been careful to count his steps when he was praying on the roof. He knew about the open skylight, but that day he forgot.

When Mihdí's mother saw how badly injured he was, her face turned white and she fainted. Although he was in great pain, Mihdí tenderly held her in his arms.

A doctor was called, but Mihdí's wounds were so bad the doctor could do nothing for him. Then 'Abdu'l-Bahá, his eyes full of tears, begged Bahá'u'lláh to heal His brother.

"O My Most Mighty Branch!" Bahá'u'lláh lovingly said to 'Abdu'l-Bahá, "leave him to his Lord."

Bahá'u'lláh was saying that they should be content with whatever was the Will of God. Mihdí's mother also went to Bahá'u'lláh. She asked Him to accept Mihdí's life as a sacrifice, but said that she wished only what Bahá'u'lláh wished.

Bahá'u'lláh asked everyone to leave Him alone with Mihdí. When everyone had left, Bahá'u'lláh asked:

"What do you wish? Tell Me."

Mihdí did not wish anything for himself. He wished only for something that would make the believers happy. He said:

"I wish that the people of Bahá will be able to attain Your presence."

Bahá'u'lláh understood what Mihdí was asking. His son wanted to die as a sacrifice in return for something good to happen. He wanted the pilgrims who came to 'Akká to be able to meet Bahá'u'lláh.

"And so it shall be," said Bahá'u'lláh. He prayed for one hour with His dearly loved son, then quietly left his bedside.

All that night and the following day Mihdí could hear Bahá'u'lláh chanting. Then Mihdí died and his radiant soul gently winged its way to the Abhá Kingdom.

29

Bahá'u'lláh Comforts Navváb

Mihdí died on 23 June in the summer of 1870. He was twenty-two years old. Everyone was very sad and his mother cried so much no-one was able to comfort her. She remembered how gentle and pure he was, and always kind and helpful; how he never complained and was loved by the friends, and was the spiritual son of his Father.

Then Bahá'u'lláh told Navváb wonderful things about the death of their son Mihdí. He said that God had accepted his death as a sacrifice so that the gates of the prison would open. This meant that the pilgrims would be able to see Bahá'u'lláh, which is what Mihdí had wished for. Bahá'u'lláh also said that because He had given His son to God, a great spiritual power had been released, and this power would help everyone in the world to be united.

When she heard these words, Navváb did not cry any more and her heart became peaceful and happy.

As Mihdí's body was being laid to rest in the ground, a faint earthquake was felt for miles around. And Bahá'u'lláh said in a prayer He revealed for Mihdí, "the earth itself trembled in its longing to meet thee."

30

A Wish Comes True

The reason why Mihdí died when he was so young is a mystery that is difficult to understand. But because he was so good and pure, God accepted his life as a gift, and his wish began to come true.

Soon after his death, the guards gradually allowed a few of the believers to visit Bahá'u'lláh in prison. Then, four months later, the gates of the prison were flung wide open. Bahá'u'lláh, His Family and the rest of the believers were taken from the prison to live in houses in other parts of 'Akká. They were still prisoners, and they still had to stay in the town, but at least the pilgrims could now visit Bahá'u'lláh.

As for Bahá'u'lláh's promise that people everywhere would become united, every day that is coming true. There are millions of people all over the world who now respect and love each other because of the teachings of Bahá'u'lláh.

31

An Important Mission

Nearly seventy years after the death of Mírzá Mihdí, Shoghi Effendi travelled by car around the bay from Haifa to 'Akká on an important mission. Shoghi Effendi was the great-grandson of Bahá'u'lláh and had been born in a house right next to the prison. When he had been a little boy, he had played in the yard under the dark shadow of the prison wall.

By this time, Mihdí's mother had grown old and also died in 'Akká, but she was buried in a different cemetery from her son. Shoghi Effendi decided that the members of Bahá'u'lláh's Family should be buried close to one another, somewhere beautiful and holy.

The place where Shoghi Effendi decided Mihdí and Navváb should be buried was on Mount Carmel, overlooking the town of Haifa. He planned to take them from the different cemeteries in 'Akká and bury them side by side amid beautiful flowers on the side of the mountain. They would then be near to the grave of Bahá'u'lláh's daughter Bahíyyih Khánum, and within sight of the Shrine of the Báb.

32

God's Holy Mountain

It was sunset on Christmas Day, 1939. Shoghi Effendi and a group of Bahá'ís were gathered on Mount Carmel. The winter sun spread rays of light across the silver coloured sea. For a few minutes, the sky was streaked with pink and red and orange light. Then everything became dark as the sun suddenly sank below the horizon.

By the light of a lamp, Shoghi Effendi lovingly carried the coffins of Mihdí and Navváb to a special spot he had prepared on the mountain. Here, he laid them to rest in two burial chambers in the ground. The chambers were built of stone, with marble floors covered in beautiful carpets. Later, a white dome was built above each grave, supported by marble pillars.

At one side of the garden, at the end of a tree-lined path and shining in the moonlight, could be seen the grave of Mihdí's sister, Bahíyyih Khánum. On the other side rose the majestic Shrine of the Báb, where 'Abdu'l-Bahá is also buried.

Shoghi Effendi covered the graves of Mihdí and Navváb with flowers, which he sprinkled with perfume of roses. Then, in his beautiful voice, he chanted prayers of thanksgiving that these beloved members of Bahá'u'lláh's Family were now buried in God's holy mountain.

Bahá'u'lláh had revealed in a prayer to His son, His beloved Mihdí:

"Thou art, verily, the trust of God and His treasure in this land." "Happy is the one that remembereth thee, and draweth nigh, through thee, unto God...."

Sources

Balyuzi, H. M., *Bahá'u'lláh, The King of Glory* (Oxford: George Ronald, 1980)

Blomfield, Lady, *The Chosen Highway* (Wilmette: Bahá'í Publishing Trust, 1940)

Faizi, A. Q., *A Gift of Love* (Gloria A. Faizi, 1982)

Ma'ani, Baharieh Rouhani, *Ásíyih Khánum, entitled The Most Exalted Leaf,* (Oxford: George Ronald, 1993)

Perkins, Mary, *Day of Glory, the Life of Bahá'u'lláh* (Oxford: George Ronald, 1992)

Salmání, Ustád Muhammad-'Alíy, *My Memories of Bahá'u'lláh* (Los Angeles: Kalimát Press, 1982)

Shoghi Effendi, *God Passes By* (Wilmette: Bahá'í Publishing Trust, 1957)

Taherzadeh, Adib, *The Revelation of Bahá'u'lláh, vol. 3* (Oxford: George Ronald, 1983)

Stories of Shoghi Effendi

Contents

"Well is it with him
that seeketh the shelter of his shade
that shadoweth all mankind."
`Abdu'l-Bahá

These stories on the life of Shoghi Effendi are lovingly dedicated to the memory of Amatu'l-Bahá Rúhíyyih Khánum. On being asked for permission to adapt material for these stories from her book *The Priceless Pearl*, Rúhíyyih Khánum graciously wrote:

"I … am glad to hear that you hope to produce something about the beloved Guardian that would be understandable for small children. I am sure that it will serve a valuable purpose. It is so important for each generation to have an understanding of the Central Figures of the Faith and the beloved Guardian, and above all, to have in their hearts love for them."

1

Shoghi Effendi

It was a peaceful day in spring, the first day of March, 1897. The sea lapped gently against the rocky shore, and tiny flowers blossomed in the cracks of the city wall that surrounded the prison-city of 'Akká. Through an open window of a house near the sea could be heard the murmur of laughter and the bustle of great excitement.

'Abdu'l-Bahá's first grandchild had just been born!

'Abdu'l-Bahá named His grandson Shoghi Effendi. Effendi means sir, or Mr, and is a title of respect. Shoghi means one who longs. 'Abdu'l-Bahá prayed that little Shoghi Effendi would always long for God.

When Shoghi Effendi was four months old, his father asked for him to be brought into the guest room, where some men friends were gathered. One by one the men looked at the sweet face of Shoghi Effendi. Then it was the turn of a Bahá'í called Dr Yúnis Khán. When the doctor looked at the baby, a feeling of wonder filled his heart. He bowed down before Shoghi Effendi and kissed the soft hair of his head.

"Only look upon him as a Bahá'í child," the doctor said to himself. But in his heart he knew that while this did make the baby very special, there was something else as well. It was not just that 'Abdu'l-Bahá was Shoghi Effendi's Grandfather. It was not even that Shoghi Effendi's father came from the Family of the Báb and his mother came from the Family of Bahá'u'lláh. Dr Yúnis Khán knew that there was a power coming from this small baby that made him different from other children.

Dr Khán knew that when Shoghi Effendi grew up he would do something very important in the world – something that had never been done before.

HOLY BIBLE

2

A Little Child Shall Lead Them

Soon after Shoghi Effendi was born, one of the believers who lived in America wrote a letter to 'Abdu'l-Bahá. She said that she had read a prophecy in the Bible which said that a little child would be the leader of the believers after 'Abdu'l-Bahá died. The lady wondered what this prophecy meant.

'Abdu'l-Bahá wrote back to the lady: "O Maidservant of God! Verily, that child is born and is alive and from him will appear wondrous things that thou wilt hear of in the future."

At the time, most of the believers were not sure whether Shoghi Effendi was the special child spoken of in the prophecy or not. A few guessed that he was, but when they asked 'Abdu'l-Bahá, He would not say. There was a good reason why 'Abdu'l-Bahá did not tell them. Most of the people were kind and faithful believers, but He knew that a few people living in 'Akká were not sincere. They only pretended to love God. If they knew how special Shoghi Effendi was, they might become jealous of him and try to harm him.

During the next few years, four more children were born into Shoghi Effendi's family. He now had two brothers and two sisters. Before long he also had nine little cousins to play with.

3

The Invisible Thread

When Shoghi Effendi was two years old, some Bahá'í pilgrims arrived from America. They came to pray in the Shrine of Bahá'u'lláh and to visit 'Abdu'l-Bahá. One of these pilgrims was called Ella. Early one morning Ella went to the room where 'Abdu'l-Bahá and the family always gathered for morning prayers, and later she described what happened.

'Abdu'l-Bahá was sitting in His favourite corner of the room next to the window. He was busy writing letters. On one side of the room a young maid sat on the floor beside a samovar, which was full of hot water for making tea. Members of 'Abdu'l-Bahá's family and the pilgrims were each given a small glass of hot, sweet tea to drink as they came into the room.

'Abdu'l-Bahá looked up from His writing. He smiled at His eldest daughter, who was Shoghi Effendi's mother, and asked her to chant a prayer. Ella described how the chanting had just finished when a small child appeared in the open doorway. It was Shoghi Effendi. He took off his shoes and came quietly into the room. He looked at 'Abdu'l-Bahá and began to walk slowly towards Him.

As Shoghi Effendi walked towards his beloved Grandfather, it seemed that he was being drawn by an invisible piece of thread. Shoghi Effendi kept his eyes on 'Abdu'l-Bahá's face, and all the time 'Abdu'l-Bahá looked lovingly at him. At last, Shoghi Effendi stood in front of 'Abdu'l-Bahá. Still looking into the eyes of his Grandfather, Shoghi Effendi reached down, lifted the hem of 'Abdu'l-Bahá's cloak and pressed it to his forehead. He kissed it, and carefully replaced it again. Then he ran out of the room to play.

4

Prayers

Shoghi Effendi loved to say prayers. One day a pilgrim asked 'Abdu'l-Bahá to write a prayer especially for children. When it was finished, Shoghi Effendi was the first to learn it by heart.

When he was very young, Shoghi Effendi kept asking his Grandfather to write him a letter.

"O My Shoghi...," wrote 'Abdu'l-Bahá at last. "Now is not the time for you to read and write, it is the time for jumping about and chanting, 'O My God!', therefore memorize the prayers of the Blessed Beauty [Bahá'u'lláh] and chant them that I may hear them...."

So Shoghi Effendi did just that. He learned as many prayers as he could and chanted them so loudly that not only 'Abdu'l-Bahá heard him, but everyone else as well! His parents told him to chant more quietly, but Shoghi Effendi said that 'Abdu'l-Bahá had told him to chant loudly so that He might hear him, and that he was doing his best!

'Abdu'l-Bahá smiled and told the grown-ups not to stop him.

5

The Courtyard

There was a courtyard and a little garden at the side of the house in 'Akká where Shoghi Effendi lived. A steep flight of steps led up from the yard to the main part of the house.

The yard was planted with a few flowers and trees and was surrounded by a high, stone wall. Next door loomed the large, grey shape of the prison. This is where Shoghi Effendi's Great-Grandfather Bahá'u'lláh and Bahá'u'lláh's Family had been imprisoned when they first arrived in 'Akká, before Shoghi Effendi was born.

Every Friday, hundreds of poor men, women and children gathered in the yard waiting for 'Abdu'l-Bahá to give them some money to buy food. Shoghi Effendi would watch his Grandfather walk down the long line of people, shaking their hands, and giving money to those who were too ill or too old to work.

At other times pilgrims would gather in the courtyard, waiting to speak to 'Abdu'l-Bahá. As they waited, they often saw little Shoghi Effendi playing on the stairs. He ran up and down the steep steps so fast that the pilgrims worried he would fall and hurt himself.

'Abdu'l-Bahá smiled and wrote something on the back of a used envelope. He wrote that Shoghi Effendi was a wise man but he ran about very much!

On another day, Shoghi Effendi went to his Grandfather's room and picked up a pen and tried to write. 'Abdu'l-Bahá drew him close so that His small grandson was standing beside Him.

"Now is not the time to write," 'Abdu'l-Bahá gently told him, "now is the time to play, you will write a lot in the future."

6

Questions

When Shoghi Effendi was about five or six years old, he was taken by his parents and great-aunt Bahíyyih Khánum to visit a town called Beirut. It was about seventy miles away from 'Akká. Although the Bahá'ís were still prisoners, the guards knew they could be trusted and did not stop them coming and going through the gates of the prison-city of 'Akká.

A Bahá'í student lived in Beirut. He was studying to be a doctor at the university. Shoghi Effendi loved to visit him. He spent hours in the student's room looking at the pictures in the books and asking questions.

In order to become a doctor, the student had to understand how all the parts of the body work. Shoghi Effendi wanted to know too. So one day the student got a dead wild cat and explained all about the different parts of the animal, and what each bit did and how everything worked. Shoghi Effendi was fascinated and watched and listened very carefully. Afterwards, the student was amazed to hear Shoghi Effendi accurately describing everything he had seen and heard.

Shoghi Effendi was so eager to learn, 'Abdu'l-Bahá had already arranged for him to have proper school lessons. One of the downstairs rooms in the house in 'Akká had been made into a classroom. 'Abdu'l-Bahá then asked a very kind, elderly Persian Bahá'í to teach Shoghi Effendi and the other children in the family. A few years later an Italian lady was paid to be their teacher. She liked Shoghi Effendi, and even when she was no longer teaching him she continued to visit him and his family. And many years later, when Shoghi Effendi married, she went to his house in Haifa to meet his wife.

7

Outings

On special, happy days, 'Abdu'l-Bahá took Shoghi Effendi and the other children for picnics in a garden outside 'Akká. It was called the Garden of Ridván. Here the air was fresh and cool away from the smells and heat of the city. 'Abdu'l-Bahá had made this garden for Bahá'u'lláh so that He could enjoy seeing green trees and beautiful flowers after having been shut up for many years in the prison in 'Akká. A stream ran through the garden and water splashed from a fountain underneath the trees. Large, juicy oranges hung on the trees, and peacocks spread their beautiful tails like fans near a summer house at the bottom of the garden.

At other times 'Abdu'l-Bahá would take his small grandson to spend the night near the Shrine of Bahá'u'lláh in a place called Bahjí, which means Delight. This was also in the country, about an hour's walk away from 'Akká.

'Abdu'l-Bahá and Shoghi Effendi would go out of the city through a gate guarded by soldiers. Then they would walk through the fields until they came to Bahjí. When they arrived, Shoghi Effendi would go with his Grandfather to a small house to wash away the dust and dirt from the journey. After they had washed, they would go into the Shrine of Bahá'u'lláh to pray.

When night came they would sleep in the house, which later became a pilgrim house and is next to the Shrine. It was very peaceful away from the noise of the town. As Shoghi Effendi settled down to sleep for the night, the only sounds to be heard were the far-off bark of a dog and the soft cooing of doves.

Then 'Abdu'l-Bahá would tuck Shoghi Effendi into bed and say, "I need him!"

8

Enemies in the Mansion

Next to the pilgrim house at Bahjí where Shoghi Effendi and 'Abdu'l-Bahá used to stay, was a large Mansion. Bahá'u'lláh had lived there during the last twelve years of His life. In the time of Bahá'u'lláh the Mansion had been clean and well-looked after. But now it was almost in ruins. The roof leaked and the whole building needed to be repaired. Someone had even plastered over the beautiful paintings on the walls of the balcony.

When he grew up, Shoghi Effendi was able to repair the Mansion so that it looked beautiful again. But when he was a child visiting the Shrine with his Grandfather, 'Abdu'l-Bahá's jealous half-brother Muhammad-'Alí was living in the Mansion with his family, and they did not look after it properly.

Muhammad-'Alí did many things that made 'Abdu'l-Bahá and Shoghi Effendi sad. In His Will, Bahá'u'lláh said that everyone should turn to 'Abdu'l-Bahá after He died, but Muhammad-'Alí disobeyed and tried to make the believers turn to him instead.

Although Muhammad-'Alí continued to do bad things, 'Abdu'l-Bahá always treated him kindly. He gave him money and food so that he and his family never needed to go hungry.

9

Danger

'Abdu'l-Bahá usually walked everywhere or rode on a donkey. But He gave His half-brother Muhammad-'Alí fine horses to ride. Muhammad-'Alí and his family liked to gallop into 'Akká, making a great deal of noise and looking rich and important.

Muhammad-'Alí was never grateful to 'Abdu'l-Bahá for His kindness. He even told lies and pretended he had no money. One of his followers went to an official in the town to complain that Muhammad-'Alí did not have money to feed his children! The official was surprised because he knew that Muhammad-'Alí had plenty of money. He knew because he was a banker and kept his money safe for him. Just two days before, this official had sent a large sum of money to Muhammad-'Alí from his bank account. Now Muhammad-'Alí was begging, saying that his children were crying with hunger! The official sent a message, telling him to use some of the money he had in his pocket to buy food for his children.

Because of the way Muhammad-'Alí was behaving, 'Abdu'l-Bahá worried in case he tried to harm Shoghi Effendi. Eventually, He decided that His young grandson would be safer if he did not continue to live in 'Akká. He sent him to the other side of the bay to live in Haifa. Shoghi Effendi's nanny went with him to look after him.

After some time, Shoghi Effendi's parents, brothers, sisters, aunts, uncles and cousins also went to live in Haifa. Several houses were built in the same street so that they could all live close to one another.

10

A Dream

Shoghi Effendi had not been living in Haifa for very long when he had a dream about bad men chasing him round a table. The Báb was also in the dream, standing on one side of the room

'Abdu'l-Bahá was still living in 'Akká at the time, but Shoghi Effendi's nanny sent someone to tell Him about His grandson's dream. As soon as He heard, 'Abdu'l-Bahá' wrote a letter to Shoghi Effendi.

"Shoghi mine," wrote 'Abdu'l-Bahá. "This dream is a very good one." He said that because Shoghi Effendi had been in the presence of His Holiness the Báb, he had been surrounded by the love and protection of God, even though people were trying to harm him.

Then 'Abdu'l-Bahá told Shoghi Effendi to be sure to do what he was asked to do in the daytime and to say prayers at night.

11

Hájar Khátún

Shoghi Effendi loved his nanny. Her name was Hájar Khátún, and she had looked after him ever since he had been a baby. She was very kind and was always there to comfort him.

When 'Abdu'l-Bahá was away on a trip, He would write letters to His family. In one letter, He told His sister, Bahíyyih Khánum, to kiss Shoghi Effendi for Him and to give greetings to Hájar Khátún.

As Shoghi Effendi grew a little older, he did not need his nanny to look after him any more, but she had become like a dear member of his family and he was very fond of her. He was very sad when his parents decided she should not live with them any more and she went away to Egypt.

Two years later Hájar Khátún died. When he heard the news, Shoghi Effendi went to a quiet part of the garden where he could be alone, and cried.

12

The Will of 'Abdu'l-Bahá

Muhammad-`Alí and some of his friends were making trouble. They told the King of Turkey that 'Abdu'l-Bahá was building a fort on Mount Carmel to fight against the King! Of course, 'Abdu'l-Bahá was not going to fight anyone. And the building He was building on the side of Mount Carmel was not a fort. It was the Shrine of the Báb. But the King did not know this and he was worried. All the Bahá'ís were worried, too, but for a different reason: they were afraid that 'Abdu'l-Bahá would be put in prison or sent away somewhere, and maybe even killed.

The only person who was not worried was 'Abdu'l-Bahá. He was very calm. He said many prayers and knew that God would make everything all right in the end. In His Will, He told the Bahá'ís what to do if He died. He said we should love one another and tell people about the teachings of Bahá'u'lláh. He also said that we should turn to Shoghi Effendi for he would be the Guardian of the Bahá'í Faith and would look after and guide us all.

When 'Abdu'l-Bahá wrote the first part of His Will, Shoghi Effendi was only nine or ten years old. To keep it safe, 'Abdu'l-Bahá hid it in a box under the ground.

13

Look at His Eyes

Shoghi Effendi had beautiful hazel eyes that sometimes seemed to change colour. At one time they looked green. At another, they looked brown. Sometimes they looked grey. At other times they looked blue.

"Look at his eyes," 'Abdu'l-Bahá would say to His wife. "They are like clear water."

A lady doctor from Germany used to visit the ladies in 'Abdu'l-Bahá's house when they were ill. She was visiting the house in Haifa one day when she met Shoghi Effendi.

'Abdu'l-Bahá saw the doctor looking at His grandson.

"How do you like my future Elisha?" asked 'Abdu'l-Bahá. By "Elisha", He meant Shoghi Effendi. Elisha was a holy man in the Bible who was a follower of the prophet Elijah. 'Abdu'l-Bahá meant that Shoghi Effendi was *His* special disciple and would carry on His work when He died.

"If I may speak openly," said the lady doctor, "I must say that in his face are the eyes of ... one who will suffer a great deal."

'Abdu'l-Bahá looked thoughtfully into the distance for some time. Then He said, "In his eyes one sees deep loyalty...."

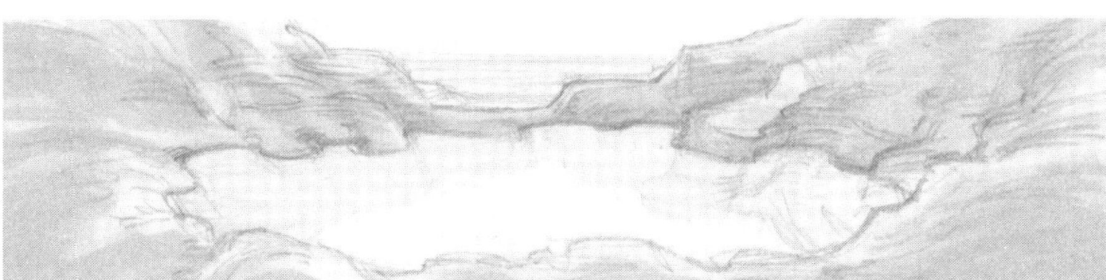

14

The Shrine of the Báb

At last 'Abdu'l-Bahá was free to leave the prison-city of 'Akká. The government said that all the people in the land who had been put in prison just because they had different ideas, could be set free.

One of the first things 'Abdu'l-Bahá did was to finish building the first part of the Shrine of the Báb on Mount Carmel, which He had begun several years before.

By Naw-Rúz, the beginning of spring, the first part of the Shrine was built. It was night and birds slept in the dark trees. Stars twinkled overhead, and a milk-white moon looked down from a purple sky. A few believers, including Shoghi Effendi, walked in the moonlight with 'Abdu'l-Bahá and entered the Shrine of the Báb.

The inside was lit by the golden glow of a lamp and soft shadows danced across the walls. 'Abdu'l-Bahá bowed down and laid His forehead on the edge of the coffin. His flowing hair shone white in the light of the lamp. Prayers were said. Then, with great love and respect, the coffin that contained the holy body of the Báb was gently laid to rest in a vault in the ground.

15

A Journey Begins

Two years after He had buried the precious remains of the Báb in the Shrine on Mount Carmel, 'Abdu'l-Bahá decided to travel to England and France to visit the Bahá'ís who lived there. People used to say that Shoghi Effendi was like his Grandfather's shadow, because everywhere 'Abdu'l-Bahá went His grandson was always with Him! But this time Shoghi Effendi had to stay behind.

However, when 'Abdu'l-Bahá returned from England and France, He decided to go on an even longer trip. He planned to go across the Atlantic Ocean to America. And this time He planned to take Shoghi Effendi with Him.

Shoghi Effendi was very excited. 'Abdu'l-Bahá stayed in Egypt during the winter, and in the spring Shoghi Effendi travelled with a few other believers from Haifa to join Him.

'Abdu'l-Bahá bought new clothes for Shoghi Effendi to wear. He ordered two turbans. One was white and the other was green. There were also some long robes. Shoghi Effendi put on the clothes and went to show 'Abdu'l-Bahá. 'Abdu'l-Bahá's eyes shone with pride when He saw how smart His grandson looked.

On 25 March 1912 they walked across the gang-plank and onto the ship that was supposed to take them on the first part of their journey to America.

16

A Journey Ends

Five other people travelled with 'Abdu'l-Bahá and Shoghi Effendi on the ship as it set sail for America. One of them was a translator. His job was to translate into English what 'Abdu'l-Bahá said in Persian. But this man was a secret enemy of 'Abdu'l-Bahá, and instead of being helpful, he caused trouble.

The ship stopped in Italy on its way to America. Here some doctors came on board to examine the passengers to make sure that none of them was ill. The doctors said that 'Abdu'l-Bahá 's cook and one of His secretaries had something wrong with their eyes. Then they said that Shoghi Effendi also had the same infection in his eyes. All three of them were ordered to leave the ship and return to Egypt.

Shoghi Effendi was surprised because he knew there was nothing wrong with his eyes. Everyone suspected that the translator had said something to the doctors to stop Shoghi Effendi being allowed to continue on the journey. 'Abdu'l-Bahá tried to find out why the doctors had said such a thing and to persuade them to change their minds, but they would not listen. Shoghi Effendi, the cook and the secretary were sent back to Egypt, and from there returned to Haifa.

When Shoghi Effendi arrived back home, another doctor examined his eyes and said that there was nothing wrong with them. His eyes were perfectly healthy.

Shoghi Effendi was heartbroken not to be with 'Abdu'l-Bahá. He became so sad that he lost his appetite and grew thin and weak. 'Abdu'l-Bahá wrote him many letters from America to cheer him up, but Shoghi Effendi had to wait more than a year before he was able to be with his beloved Grandfather again.

17

With 'Abdu'l-Bahá Again

'Abdu'l-Bahá returned to Egypt from America in the summer of 1913. As soon as possible, Shoghi Effendi, with his great-aunt Bahíyyih Khánum and others, went to Egypt to be with Him.

'Abdu'l-Bahá was now almost seventy years old. He had been travelling and giving talks at meetings nearly every day when He was in America, and He was very tired. He also had a fever and needed to rest, so He decided to stay in Egypt until He felt well again.

Shoghi Effendi helped in many ways. Sometimes he worked as 'Abdu'l-Bahá's secretary. 'Abdu'l-Bahá would sit in a shady part of the garden out of the sun and dictate letters in Persian. Shoghi Effendi would write down whatever 'Abdu'l-Bahá was saying and then send the letters to the believers.

Sometimes 'Abdu'l-Bahá sent him to meet the Bahá'í pilgrims when they arrived at the railway station, and once 'Abdu'l-Bahá asked him to take some of the friends to the zoo. He also went to Cairo and probably saw the pyramids.

Early in the morning, the friends often heard Shoghi Effendi chanting prayers, and 'Abdu'l-Bahá teaching him how to chant even more beautifully.

The days passed happily by and Shoghi Effendi wished he could stay with 'Abdu'l-Bahá in Egypt for ever. But before long the summer holidays came to an end and he had to return to school.

18

School

When Shoghi Effendi first went to school in Haifa he was not happy there. We don't know why, but he became very sad. Of course, most schools were very strict in those days and not so friendly as they are now. It seems there were no other suitable schools in Haifa at that time, so after a while he went to a boarding school in the town of Beruit, which was quite a long way away. The family hoped he would be happier there. But although he was clever and did well at his lessons, Shoghi Effendi still felt sad. For one thing, he was even further away from his beloved Grandfather, 'Abdu'l-Bahá!

'Abdu'l-Bahá decided to send one of the believers to look after Shoghi Effendi so that he could stay in a house and not have to live in the school. But this believer soon wrote saying that Shoghi Effendi was still very thin and was not eating enough, and she was very worried about him.

Eventually, 'Abdu'l-Bahá arranged for Shoghi Effendi to go to another school in Beirut. This one was also part of a college for older students. Later, this college became known as the American University and students came to study there from many different countries.

At the college there were other Bahá'í students. Shoghi Effendi used to meet with them to talk about the Bahá'í teachings. They talked about how they could help the Bahá'ís who lived in other countries, and decided to spend their spare time writing to these friends to give them news of what was happening in the Holy Land.

19

During the War

A world war began in 1914. Some of the Bahá'í students at the university in Beirut, where Shoghi Effendi was studying, came from Persia. Because of the fighting it was impossible for them to travel home in the holidays. Instead, they often stayed in Haifa. One of these friends travelled on horseback all the way, galloping for miles over the fields and along the seashore until he came to Mount Carmel and the little town of Haifa.

The students loved being with Shoghi Effendi. He was always cheerful and full of hope. He told them not to worry and that one day the teachings of Bahá'u'lláh would spread to every country, and then there would be peace in the world.

The war lasted for four years and the shops often ran out of food. Whenever they could, Shoghi Effendi's family sent him food parcels of nuts, dried fruit, honey and bread, which Shoghi Effendi shared with one of his friends. Back in Haifa, `Abdu'l-Bahá arranged for wheat and barley to be brought from Bahá' farms in other parts of the country, and thousands of people were fed who otherwise would have died of hunger.

One day, Shoghi Effendi managed to buy some cheese in Beirut. He knew that it was almost impossible to buy cheese in Haifa because of the war, so he sent it as a treat for `Abdu'l-Bahá.

20

After the War

The war caused a great deal of suffering. Thousands of people died in the battles, and thousands more died of hunger. Once, cannons were fired at Haifa, but fortunately all the cannon balls missed the houses and just splashed into the sea.

By the time the war ended, Shoghi Effendi had finished his education at the university and returned home to live in Haifa. He was very happy because he was able to help 'Abdu'l-Bahá by being His secretary. Some of the letters he wrote were printed in a magazine called *Star of the West*, which was a magazine for the Bahá'ís in the West. This magazine was printed mainly in English, but Shoghi Effendi could speak many languages. As well as English, he could read and write in Persian, Arabic, Turkish and French.

Shoghi Effendi's bedroom was next to 'Abdu'l-Bahá's. Shoghi Effendi often worked late into the night and 'Abdu'l-Bahá would see the light shining under his bedroom door. He would call out to Shoghi Effendi, "Enough! Enough! Go to sleep!" But He was pleased that His grandson was so serious about doing his work.

For the next two years Shoghi Effendi was with 'Abdu'l-Bahá almost every day. Together they met followers of different religions and important people from the government. Shoghi Effendi noticed how lovingly 'Abdu'l-Bahá treated people, and how polite He was to everyone.

21

England

'Abdu'l-Bahá' decided that Shoghi Effendi should continue his education and go to university in England. Shoghi Effendi was happy to go because he knew this would help him to improve his English and he would be able to translate the Writings of Bahá'u'lláh more beautifully.

He arrived in England in July 1920 and was met by the Bahá'ís. Some of them had met 'Abdu'l-Bahá when He had visited England and Scotland some years before and they were very pleased to meet His grandson.

Shoghi Effendi already knew at least one of the British believers. This was a young Scottish doctor named John Esslemont. Dr Esslemont had come to Haifa on pilgrimage, and he and Shoghi Effendi had become good friends. When he was in England, Shoghi Effendi visited the seaside town of Bournemouth, where Dr Esslemont was working in a hospital, and spent a few days with him.

Shoghi Effendi became a student at Balliol College at Oxford University. The university was very old and surrounded with large trees and peaceful parks. A river flowed nearby, and there the students walked together and talked about their studies. Shoghi Effendi worked hard and was always asking his teachers questions. He also translated some of the Writings of Bahá'u'lláh into English. One of the Tablets he translated at this time was a letter which Bahá'u'lláh had written to Queen Victoria.

Whenever he could, Shoghi Effendi went to the Bahá'í meetings and gave talks about the Faith. He visited famous places like the British Museum and the Houses of Parliament.

Many years later, he told a pilgrim how much he had enjoyed eating thick slices of brown bread with raspberry jam and cream when he was a young student in England!

22

The Passing of 'Abdu'l-Bahá

Shoghi Effendi spent one year in England. During that time, 'Abdu'l-Bahá, Who was still living in Haifa, had two strange dreams. 'Abdu'l-Bahá knew that these dreams were telling Him that His work in this world would soon come to an end and the time had come for Him to go to the next world. He did not tell His family the meaning of the dreams because He did not want them to feel sad. But when He became ill, He asked them to send a cable to Shoghi Effendi telling him to return immediately.

The family did not realise how ill 'Abdu'l-Bahá was. They should have obeyed Him at once and sent the telegram, but they wrote a letter instead. They thought that if Shoghi Effendi suddenly received a telegram he would become very worried. The letter arrived two weeks later, but by that time 'Abdu'l-Bahá had died.

When he heard the sad news, Shoghi Effendi got such a shock that he became ill. A Bahá'í called Miss Grand who lived in London looked after him for a few days. Then Shoghi Effendi's friend John Esslemont wrote him a letter inviting him to stay with him for a few days in Bournemouth, which was beside the sea.

"Dearest Shoghi ...," Dr Esslemont wrote. "It must be very hard for you, away from your family ... you are most welcome to come here for a few days.... Just send me a wire ... and I shall have a room ready for you."

Shoghi Effendi accepted Dr Esslemont's kind invitation. While he was in Bournemouth, he wrote letters to his other Bahá'í friends. He knew they were heart-broken too because 'Abdu'l-Bahá had passed away.

23

A Surprise in Haifa

One of the people Shoghi Effendi wrote to when he first heard the news that 'Abdu'l-Bahá had died was Mr Hall, a believer who lived in Manchester, in the north of England. Mr Hall replied at once, sending love from all the Bahá'ís who lived in Manchester. He wrote: "... we all love you dearly, and we are all united and stronger than ever."

With these words in his heart, Shoghi Effendi left England to return to the Holy Land.

He travelled by ship to Egypt, and then by train to Haifa. The journey took two weeks, and when he arrived he was so overcome with grief at the passing of his beloved Grandfather that he could hardly walk up the steps to the house. His great-aunt Bahíyyih Khánum made sure that he had a good rest, and then he was told about 'Abdu'l-Bahá's Will.

In His Will, 'Abdu'l-Bahá said He had chosen Shoghi Effendi to be the Guardian of the Bahá'í Faith.

24

The Guardian

'Abdu'l-Bahá's Will was very clear. Shoghi Effendi was now the Guardian who would look after the Cause of God and guide the Bahá'ís. He could also tell the believers what the Writings of the Báb, Bahá'u'lláh and 'Abdu'l-Bahá meant. If anyone was not sure about something they should ask Shoghi Effendi.

"O my loving friends!" 'Abdu'l-Bahá had written. "After the passing away of this wronged one,... turn unto Shoghi Effendi as he is the sign of God, the chosen branch, the Guardian of the Cause of God...."

'Abdu'l-Bahá wrote something else in His Will that was very important. He said that one day the Universal House of Justice would be elected. He promised that both the Universal House of Justice and the Guardian would always be under the care and protection of the Báb and Bahá'u'lláh from the Abhá Kingdom, and that they would always be guided to know the right thing to do.

"Whatever they decide," wrote 'Abdu'l-Bahá, "is of God."

'Abdu'l-Bahá had known that this new work Shoghi Effendi had to do would be difficult. He would need to translate more of the Writings of Bahá'u'lláh into English. He would need to make sure that the Writings were also translated into hundreds of other languages so that everyone in the world would be able to read them. He would need to make sure that everyone on earth would eventually hear the wonderful teachings of Bahá'u'lláh. He would need to help the Bahá'ís form National and Local Spiritual

Assemblies in every country. He would need to write thousands of letters, and answer thousands of different questions. He would need to finish building the Shrine of the Báb, which did not have a dome on it yet, and he would need to plant beautiful gardens on Mount Carmel and around the Shrine of Bahá'u'lláh.

In His Will, 'Abdu'l-Bahá asked the Bahá'ís to look after Shoghi Effendi.

"O ye the faithful ones of 'Abdu'l-Bahá!" He wrote, "...take the greatest care of Shoghi Effendi ... that day by day he may ... grow to become even as a fruitful tree."

25

Tests

Shoghi Effendi was only twenty-four years old when he became the Guardian of the Bahá'í Faith. However, although he was such a young man, he knew what he had to do, and 'Abdu'l-Bahá had promised that the Báb and Bahá'u'lláh would help him from the next world.

Bahá'ís from around the world wrote to Shoghi Effendi, sending their love and saying how pleased they were that he was the Guardian. But in the Holy Land, where Shoghi Effendi lived, some enemies made life very difficult for him. Muhammad-'Alí, the same half-brother of 'Abdu'l-Bahá who had always been troublesome and had disobeyed Bahá'u'lláh many times before, now caused more trouble. With others, he stole the keys to the Shrine of Bahá'u'lláh. This meant that none of the Bahá'ís could go into the Shrine to pray.

Government officials then took the keys and kept them while the matter was taken to court. Month after month passed by and the door to the Shrine remained locked. At last, after eight months, a judge said that the keys should be returned to Shoghi Effendi. Shoghi Effendi was very thankful that his prayers had been answered, but he became ill because he was so sad that anyone could have done such a terrible thing as to steal the keys to the Holy Shrine of Bahá'u'lláh. He decided to go somewhere quiet, away from all the troubles, where he could spend his time praying to God, go for long walks in the countryside, and rest until he felt well and strong again.

Shoghi Effendi's great-aunt Bahíyyih Khánum understood and did everything she could to help him. Shoghi Effendi said that she was not just a friend to all of us, but she was like a mother. He knew that she would look after things while he was away.

First of all he went to Germany to see a good doctor. Then he took a long train journey to a small town in Switzerland which was surrounded by mountains.

26

Peaceful Mountains

When Shoghi Effendi was in Switzerland he rented a room in a small house. His room was in the attic and it had a very low ceiling. Tall people had to be careful not to bump their heads when they went to visit him. But he was happy staying in this simple house, and he became very friendly with the owner and his wife.

Most days, Shoghi Effendi got up early in the morning while it was still dark. There was no way to heat the water so he washed in cold water, then quietly left the house without waking anyone. He walked down the road to the railway station and travelled a short distance by train until he reached the foot of the mountains.

He walked all day over the mountains, and, apart from a guide who sometimes went with him, he hardly ever met anyone. It often rained and he got soaking wet. When the rain stopped, the wind dried his clothes. When he reached a high peak, he rested, and gazed over the snowy tops of the mountains and down to the green valleys below. He loved the peaceful scenery. Some years later he sent money to the Bahá'ís in Switzerland so they could buy a piece of land where a Bahá'í Temple will be built one day.

After a few months, Shoghi Effendi felt strong and well again and returned to Haifa. The very next day he wrote to all the Bahá'í communities in the world. He sent his love and promised to help them in every way he could.

27
The Wish

Although she was now very frail, Bahíyyih Khánum continued to help Shoghi Effendi. In the evenings, Shoghi Effendi would go to her room and they would have their meal together. He loved to sit with her and hear stories of the days when she had been a little girl living in Persia. Sometimes he would ask the Bahá'í youth to read poems and sing for her. He was always doing little things to make her happy.

The day came when Bahíyyih Khánum died. It was time for her soul to go to the Abhá Kingdom. Shoghi Effendi was away at the time but he had prepared a special place on the side of Mount Carmel for her grave. When he returned, he held a meeting where people were invited to speak about her wonderful life and read poems they had written about her. A hundred poor people were also fed on that day.

Before she died, Bahíyyih Khánum told Shoghi Effendi about a wish she had in her heart. She wished to be buried near to her mother, Navváb. Shoghi Effendi did not forget her wish. A few years after Bahíyyih Khánum's funeral, he arranged for the remains of Navváb to be brought from the cemetery in 'Akká to be buried close to her daughter's grave on Mount Carmel. He also brought the remains of the Purest Branch to be buried on the mountain with them.

Shoghi Effendi sent a telegram to the Bahá'ís of the world telling them that Bahíyyih Khánum's wish had come true.

28

Bahá'í Schools

In Persia there were several Bahá'í schools. Two of them were in the capital city of Tihrán. They were called Tarbiyat Schools. Tarbiyat means training. One was for girls and the other for boys. Not only Bahá'í children went to them, but other children too. Even the King of Persia sent his son to the boy's school because it was the best one in the country.

On Bahá'í Holy Days the Bahá'í schools closed because Bahá'u'lláh said that we should not work on these special days. But one year the government ordered that the schools should stay open. The Bahá'ís in Persia wrote to Shoghi Effendi asking what they should do. Should they obey the government and keep the schools open on the next Holy Day? Or should they obey Bahá'u'lláh and close the schools?

Shoghi Effendi told them to obey Bahá'u'lláh and close the schools on that day.

The next Holy Day was in memory of the Martyrdom of the Báb. The schools stayed closed and the children stayed at home. The government authorities were not pleased. They sent a letter to the Bahá'ís saying that the schools would never be allowed to open again.

Shoghi Effendi had known this would happen, but he knew that we must always obey Bahá'u'lláh. He also knew something the government did not know: he knew that one day there would be many Bahá'í schools, not just in Persia, but all over the world.

29

The Happy Gardens (1)

When Shoghi Effendi had first gone to live in Haifa, the mountain behind it was almost bare, with just a few small bushes dotted over its steep sides. Weeds and wild flowers tried to grow in the thin soil, and every time it rained more earth was washed down to the sea. The holy Shrine of the Báb had been built on the mountain, but the ground around it was still rocky and wild.

Now Shoghi Effendi decided to make a beautiful garden around the Shrine of the Báb. First of all, He cleared away the stones and planted grass seed. An old gardener who was watching shook his head and said that it was impossible to make beautiful lawns on the mountain. It was too dry and hard. But Shoghi Effendi kept on trying and, at last, he found the right kind of seed that would grow well on the mountainside. Before long, bright green grass was spreading like a smile over Mount Carmel.

It was even more difficult to grow flowers and make a garden. Shoghi Effendi ordered thousands of bulbs from Holland, but all of them died. He ordered hundreds of rose bushes from France, but they did not grow either. Even with all these difficulties, he never gave up. He brought lorry loads of earth to cover the ground and tried growing many different kinds of flowers until he found ones that were happy living on the mountain.

Before long, the land around the Shrine of the Báb was full of different coloured roses, red geraniums, blue jacaranda, white honeysuckle, purple bougainvillaea, and trees covered in orange blossom.

30

The Happy Gardens (2)

Shoghi Effendi also began planting gardens around the Shrine of Bahá'u'lláh in Bahji. The land is flat in Bahji, not steep like on the mountain in Haifa. 'Abdu'l-Bahá had already planted some flowers there and now Shoghi Effendi wanted to make the gardens bigger. With long pieces of string, he marked out where the flowerbeds and paths should be. The gardeners walked behind him as he explained what needed to be done. If pilgrims were visiting, then they helped too.

There was an old, one-roomed building on the edge of the land at Bahji. One day, Shoghi Effendi climbed onto the flat roof and found that he could see the whole of the garden. This gave him a good idea. When the garden was finished, he used earth that had been dug up by a bulldozer to make a small hill. Later, this was made even bigger when some old buildings were knocked down and they were added to the hill, covered with earth, and grass and flowers planted on top. From this hill, you can see the garden spreading in all directions, like a beautifully patterned carpet made of flowers.

By this time, the enemies of the Faith no longer lived in the Mansion at Bahji. Shoghi Effendi was now able to have the roof repaired, and an artist repainted the lovely pictures on the walls of the balcony.

Inside, Shoghi Effendi made the Mansion like a museum, full of pictures and books and other interesting things. This was the House where Bahá'u'lláh had lived for twelve years and where He passed away. Shoghi Effendi kept Bahá'u'lláh's room looking as much as possible as it had looked when He lived there. One of Bahá'u'lláh's hats, called a táj, was often placed on a couch in the corner where He sometimes sat. And His slippers were placed on the floor beside a bed.

Thousands of people visit the beautiful Bahá'í Holy Places. One lady wrote a letter to Shoghi Effendi when she returned to her home. She said how much she had enjoyed the quiet beauty of the Shrines and the happiness of the gardens.

31
A Wedding

A young girl named Mary Maxwell was on pilgrimage with her mother and father. Some years before, 'Abdu'l-Bahá had prayed for Mr and Mrs Maxwell to have a child, and then Mary had been born. When she was a baby, 'Abdu'l-Bahá visited her home in Canada and held her in His arms. Now Mary was twelve years old, and she was on pilgrimage with her parents. It was a Holy Day, the Ascension of Bahá'u'lláh, and they had been in the Shrine of Bahá'u'lláh and the Mansion of Bahjí praying all night.

It was dawn when Shoghi Effend, Mr and Mrs Maxwell and Mary drove back to Haifa. They rode in an open top car along the seashore. There was no road built around the bay at that time so people had to travel in cars or horse-drawn carriages over the sand. Instead of sitting on the seat, Mary was perched on the folded hood of the car at the back, watching hundreds of tiny white crabs running across the sand. Shoghi Effendi told her to be careful not to fall off! As the sun's rays lit up the sky, Mary thought how "fresh and rosy and clean" everything looked. Shoghi Effendi also enjoyed being in the open air, and he told Mary how he loved to climb mountains.

Fourteen more years passed by and Mary grew up. She returned twice to visit the Holy Shrines in Haifa and Bahjí, once with friends and once with her mother. On the last visit, Shoghi Effendi said he had chosen her to be his wife. He gave her his Bahá'í ring, which had been given to him by his great-aunt Bahíyyih Khánum. Mary wore the ring on a ribbon round her neck until the day she was married.

The day of the wedding arrived. Shoghi Effendi and Mary went first of all to the Shrine of Bahá'u'lláh and chanted prayers. Shoghi Effendi asked Mary to give him the ring, and he put it on her finger. Then they returned to Haifa and went to the room which had been Bahíyyih Khánum's when she was alive. There they said their marriage vows: "We will all, verily, abide by the Will of God."

Shoghi Effendi gave Mary a new name when they were married. He named her Amatu'l-Bahá Rúhíyyih Khánum. Amatu'l-Bahá means the maidservant of Bahá'u'lláh. Rúhíyyih means spiritual. Khánum is a title of respect and means lady.

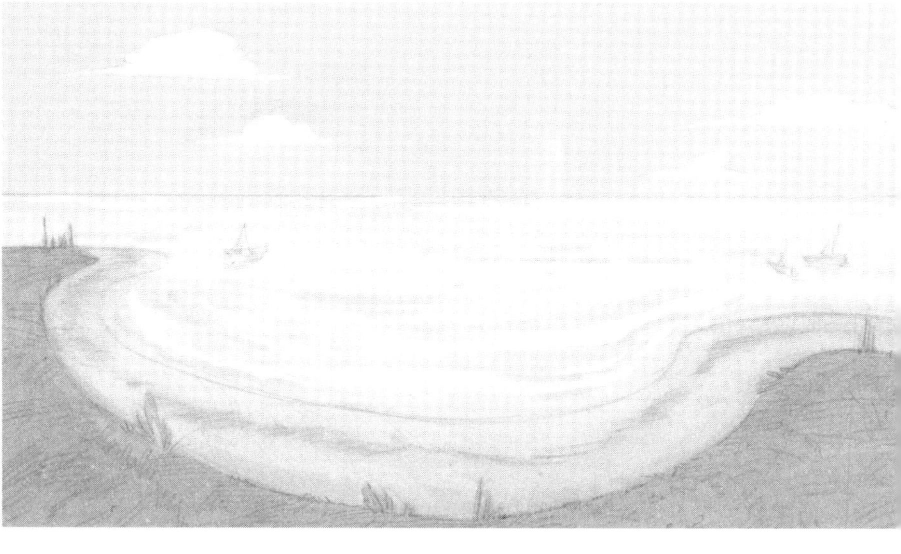

32

A Dangerous Journey

One day, to everyone's surprise, Shoghi Effendi said he was going to travel to England. They were surprised because it was 1940 and a world war had just started, and it was almost impossible to travel to other countries. Not only was it very dangerous, but it was very difficult to get permission to travel. And most of the passenger ships were being used in the war, so even if people did get permission, they often could not go anywhere.

Shoghi Effendi had to get something called a visa, as this would allow him to enter England, so he sent a letter off to London. The days and weeks passed by but the visa did not arrive. Finally, he decided to start his journey anyway and hope that he could get a visa on the way.

Shoghi Effendi and Rúhíyyih Khánum travelled on the first part of the journey on an aquaplane, which was like a raft towed by a motorboat. The water seeped up between the boards and underneath their feet. The aquaplane was small and smelly and very uncomfortable, but at last they arrived in Italy. Here they met up with Rúhíyyih Khánum's father, Mr Sutherland Maxwell, who had come from Canada. Mr Maxwell's wife had died and Shoghi Effendi had invited him to come to Haifa to live.

In Italy, Shoghi Effendi asked Rúhíyyih Khánum and her father to see a man called a Consul, who was a representative of the British Government in Italy, and ask for a visa for England.

They set off at once and found the office, but the Consul said that he had no authority to give a visa and that it could only be done through the government in London.

Disappointed, Rúhíyyih Khánum and her father returned to Shoghi Effendi and told him what had happened.

But Shoghi Effendi told them to go back and try again! They did not know what else they could say, but, of course, they obeyed the Guardian and returned to the office. They sat opposite the Consul and repeated everything they had said before, telling him that Shoghi Effendi was the Head of the Bahá'í Faith and it was very important that he had a visa so that he could go to London. Then Rúhíyyih Khánum just happened to say that Shoghi Effendi was the grandson of 'Abdu'l-Bahá. The Consul looked at her and said, "I remember 'Abdu'l-Bahá!" He had met the Master many years ago and his heart had been touched by His love.

Without saying anything more, the Consul took Shoghi Effendi's passport and stamped a visa for England in it. He said that he had no authority to do it and it may not be accepted when they got to England, but they could take a chance and see what happened.

Immediately, Shoghi Effendi, Rúhíyyih Khánum and Mr Maxwell left Italy and travelled to France, on the next part of their journey. A few days after they left, Italy joined the countries that were at war with Britain. If Shoghi Effendi had still been in Italy, he probably would not have been able to leave the country at all.

From France they managed to get one of the last two boats that were taking passengers across the sea to England. After these boats left, all the ports were closed and no more boats were allowed to leave.

The very next day, enemy soldiers marched into the town where Shoghi Effendi and the rest of the family had been staying in France. However, by that time, they had safely arrived in England.

What Shoghi Effendi did in London is a mystery. But whatever it was, when it was done, they began their journey back home, and this was even more exciting than their first journey.

Because France and Italy were now at war with each other, they could not go back to the Holy Land the way they had come. The only way to get back to Haifa was a very long and roundabout way through Africa. So they set sail on a ship that was going to South Africa.

Instead of sailing in a straight line, the captain made the boat zig-zag from side to side so that the sailors in the enemy submarines under the water would be confused and not know exactly where to aim their torpedoes!

After many weeks the ship sailed into a harbour in South Africa, and Shoghi Effendi and Rúhíyyih Khánum travelled overland to Egypt and then back to Haifa. Mr Maxwell went by plane as far as Egypt, because Shoghi Effendi was worried about his health.

Six months after Shoghi Effendi and Rúhíyyih Khánum had first left the Holy Land, they arrived safely back home again.

33

Shoghi Effendi's Book

The war lasted for six years. No Bahá'í pilgrims were able to visit the Holy Land during that time because it was too dangerous to travel. Ships were being sunk by submarines, and roads and railway lines were being blown up by bombs.

During this time when there were no visitors, Shoghi Effendi began to write a book. He had already translated many of the Writings of Bahá'u'lláh, and translated a large book called *The Dawn-Breakers*, which is full of adventure stories about the first people who believed in the Báb. Now he decided to write a book about the history of the first one hundred years of the Bahá'í Faith. He called his book *God Passes By*. Shoghi Effendi planned to finish his book by 1944, which was exactly one hundred years after the Báb declared that He was a Manifestation of God.

People did not have computers in those days. First, Shoghi Effendi wrote his book by hand. Then he typed it out on a small typewriter. With Rúhíyyih Khánum's help, he added hundreds of little accents on top of the Persian and Arabic names, often working late into the night.

While Shoghi Effendi was busy writing, there was fighting going on in the streets around the house where he and Rúhíyyih Khánum lived. One day a fighter plane crashed nearby and burst into flames. But nothing stopped Shoghi Effendi from doing his work, and in 1944 the book was finished and sent to America to be printed.

34

Battle in the Streets

A year after Shoghi Effendi finished writing his book, one war ended but another one began! This time, the war was just in the Holy Land. Many people ran away from the fighting, but Shoghi Effendi and Rúhíyyih Khánum stayed in Haifa.

Every afternoon, Shoghi Effendi went up Mount Carmel to pray in the Shrine of the Báb. He also supervised the work in the gardens. One day when he was driving up the mountain, people in two cars behind him began shooting at each other. Bullets were flying everywhere! Then one of the cars overtook the car Shoghi Effendi was travelling in, so, for a while, his car was trapped between the two.

On another day, soldiers put a machine gun in the Bahá'í gardens, pointing at the road. Shoghi Effendi asked the authorities to move it at once, which they did. But as it became too dangerous to drive on the road, he walked up the mountain to the Shrine instead.

Shoghi Effendi prayed that God would keep the Shrines safe, and his prayers were answered. Although gun battles continued to take place around Haifa and 'Akká, the Shrines of the Báb and Bahá'u'lláh were never hit.

35

Three Crowns

Shoghi Effendi decided to complete the Shrine where the Báb was buried and which 'Abdu'l-Bahá had begun many years before. At that time, the Shrine was just a square building and Shoghi Effendi wanted to surround it with beautiful pillars and place a glorious dome on top.

The finished Shrine looks like three crowns. The first crown is set on top of twenty-four rose-coloured pillars. This crown is made of marble and decorated with carvings of green leaves and red flowers. One day, Writings of the Báb in Arabic will be engraved on it. In the front of the crown, like a beautiful jewel, is the symbol of the Greatest Name, Ya Bahá'u'l-Abhá. It means "O Thou the Glory of the Most Glorious" and is another Name for Bahá'u'lláh.

The second crown is above the first one, and has a ring of eight dainty spires around it, each one like a small graceful minaret tipped with gold. When the sun shines, they look like lighted candles.

On top of this is a circle of eighteen very tall, narrow windows with patterns of flowers on them. They remind us of the first eighteen believers in the Báb, who were called the Letters of the Living.

Above these windows, the third crown is a band of marble, on top of which is a magnificent golden dome.

But before he could begin to build the Shrine, Shoghi Effendi had to find the right kinds of materials. He had to find a quarry somewhere in the world that had rose-coloured granite to make the pillars which would be put around the square part of the Shrine. Then he had to find another quarry with perfect white marble to make the crowns.

The Shrine of the Báb was going to be one of the most beautiful buildings in the world.

36

The Shrine is Finished

Rúhíyyih Khánum's father, Mr Sutherland Maxwell, was an excellent architect. He had designed many important buildings in Canada, where he used to live. He was very excited when Shoghi Effendi asked him to help design the final parts of the Shrine of the Báb. Mr Maxwell also designed dainty patterns of leaves and flowers to be carved on top of the pillars and around the three crowns on the Shrine.

Because a war was still being fought in the Holy Land, it was not possible to buy the materials that were needed for the building work. So Shoghi Effendi sent Mr Maxwell and another believer to Italy to try to find the granite and marble that was needed. There they met Dr Ugo Giachery, who lived in Italy, and they began to search all over the country to find the right kind of quarries, and workmen skilled enough to do the carving.

Eventually they found a firm able to do the work. The granite was taken out of the ground in enormous blocks, and then sixty sculptors began carving them into twenty-four pillars. All the time this was going on, telegrams were being sent between Haifa and Italy and Shoghi Effendi was guiding everything that was happening.

At last, the carefully cut marble and the granite pillars were packed in large wooden crates. These were then put into second crates to be sent to Haifa. On the way to Haifa, one of the cargo boats carrying the marble for the Shrine stopped at another port to pick up bags of soot, which a factory needed for making black paint. Because the boat was already full, the bags of soot were put on top of the crates that had the white marble inside.

During the journey there was a storm. The waves tossed the boat from side to side and most of the bags of soot burst open. The black dust seeped through the outer crates, and everyone was worried that it had stained the white marble inside.

In Haifa, Shoghi Effendi was waiting anxiously for the boats to arrive. When they sailed into the harbour he was very relieved and watched as a crane lifted the heavy crates off the boats. Large lorries then took the crates up the mountain to where the Shrine was being built. There, the wooden crates were unpacked. The white marble was all right! Because it had been packed so well, in two crates instead of just one, none of the soot had seeped through to spoil it.

The graceful pillars were carefully put up around the square part of the Shrine. Then the three crowns were placed, one on top of the other. The gold-coloured dome rose like a sun on top of the holy Shrine of the Báb. Altogether, from the beginning to the end, the last part of the Shrine had taken five years to build.

Shoghi Effendi said that the Shrine was like a Queen and Mount Carmel was her Throne; and that she was dressed in a white robe, and had a crown of glowing gold.

37

The Beautiful Gate

From time to time, there were other special people who came to stay in Haifa to help Shoghi Effendi with the work that had to be done. One of them was a Bahá'í named Mrs Amelia Collins. Everyone called her Milly. She was very kind and Shoghi Effendi loved her very much.

When Milly was a little girl, she longed to have a beautiful gate! She did not want a wooden one; she wanted a fancy one made by hammering black iron into lovely shapes. Perhaps she had seen such a gate in a book, or leading into an important building. She spent hours trying to make a gate out of small pieces of wire and tin for her doll's house. But she could never make anything that seemed good enough.

Even when Milly was grown up she still dreamed of one day having this special gate. When she married, her husband asked if she would like a gate of wrought iron to be made for the garden of their new house. However, when Milly heard how much it would cost, she thought it was far too expensive and told her husband not to have one made after all.

The years passed by and Milly heard about Bahá'u'lláh and His wonderful teachings and became a Bahá'í. And she forgot all about the gate.

Although Milly did not spend much money on herself, she was very generous and gave a lot of her money away to other people. Once, she gave enough money to the Fund to buy the land on top of Mount Carmel where Bahá'u'lláh had walked and where a Temple will be built one day. She was also the very

first Bahá'í to give money to help build the dome on the Shrin of the Báb. She was always sending money to help poor Nationa Spiritual Assemblies around the world. She did not tell every one around her when she gave her money away. But Shogh Effendi knew how humble and kind she was.

Milly wanted to give something to Shoghi Effendi – somethin that would be just for him. She knew he never spent money o himself, so she gave him some as a present.

Some time later, Milly received a letter from Shoghi Effendi Inside the letter was a photograph of a beautiful gate! Th main part was made of long, slim rods of shiny black iron, s that people could look through and see what was beyond. I felt as smooth as silk when you touched it with your finger. I was higher than the tallest man and wide enough for ten peopl to pass through at the same time. Across the top, in a curve was a dainty design, and above that were some twirly bits an patterns of leaves. And in the centre, above everyone's head was the symbol of the Greatest Name, Bahá'u'lláh.

Milly could not believe her eyes. Here was the gate of he dreams. When she read the letter, she learned that Shogh Effendi had not after all bought anything for himself with th money she had given him. Instead, He had used it to make thi beautiful gate in the gardens at Bahjí. And he had put it in a special place, at the entrance to the white pebbled path tha leads to the Shrine of Bahá'u'lláh.

It is called "The Collins Gate", in memory of Milly.

38

The Hands of the Cause of God

Shoghi Effendi sent an exciting message to the Bahá'ís around the world. He had decided to call some of the believers Hands of the Cause of God. We all need our own hands to do things, and these believers were chosen to do especially important work for God. They helped the Bahá'ís to understand and obey the teachings of Bahá'u'lláh, to be united and happy, and to love one another.

Only Bahá'u'lláh, `Abdu'l-Bahá and Shoghi Effendi were able to appoint Hands of the Cause, so there can never be any more. Some of the Hands were named after they had died. Others, while they were still alive.

The Hands of the Cause were very humble. They were very surprised when Shoghi Effendi wrote saying they had been given this great honour. One of the Hands thought the message must be for his wife, not for him. He said that she was much better than he was, so it must be for her! But Shoghi Effendi lovingly told him that it was meant for him. Others cried when they heard, because they did not feel they were good enough. All of them spent many days praying, asking God to help them in the important work they had to do.

We know the names of at least 50 Hands of the Cause. One of them was Mrs Amelia Collins. Another was Rúhiyyih Khánum's father, Mr Sutherland Maxwell, and, after he died, Rúhíyyih Khánum herself. Dr Ugo Giachery, who lived in Italy, was another. All of the Hands were very special people. The next story is about one of them. He had lived in the time of

Bahá'u'lláh, 'Abdu'l-Bahá, Shoghi Effendi, and the Universal House of Justice. His name was Tarázu'lláh Samandarí.

39

A Shining Lamp

Mr Tarázu'lláh Samandarí was born in the time of Bahá'u'lláh. When he was sixteen years old, he travelled with his mother and sister and a few of the Bahá'ís from Persia to visit Bahá'u'lláh in the Holy Land. He arrived in the spring, at the time of Naw-Rúz. Bahá'u'lláh welcomed him and gave him a present of some new clothes: a silk robe to wear under his outer one, a shirt, a long cloth to tie around his waist, and a pair of socks.

Young Tarázu'lláh stayed seven months in 'Akká, and whenever he could he went to Bahji to be with Bahá'u'lláh. Because there were so many people, meetings were often held in a large tent in the garden. Once, the only place left for Tarázu'lláh to sit down was by the door, at the opposite side of the room to where Bahá'u'lláh was. Tarázu'lláh did not want to be so far away – he wanted to be as close as possible to Bahá'u'lláh, so he ran round to the back of the tent, where there was a space the size of a cupboard, which was used as a store. Here, he was right next to Bahá'u'lláh and could clearly hear what He said, even though he could not see Him on the other side of the canvas wall of the tent.

At the end of the meeting a tray of oranges was passed round. Bahá'u'lláh took an orange and told everyone else to take one as well. Tarázu'lláh was worried in case there would be none left for him, especially as no-one knew he was there! He ran round the outside of the tent and stood just inside the door, with his arms folded and his eyes humbly looking at the ground. As Bahá'u'lláh left the tent, He stopped by Tarázu'lláh – and gave him the orange He had taken for Himself!

Some of the other youth teased Tarázu'lláh and tried to take the orange away from him, even though they had their own. But Tarázu'lláh ran away from them. This was no ordinary orange, he thought, as he dodged round corners so the boys could not catch him: this orange Bahá'u'lláh had given to him with His own hands!

What Tarázu'lláh loved most of all was to hear Bahá'u'lláh chanting the Holy Words of God. As he listened, his heart became full of happiness.

When Tarázu'lláh Samandarí was about seventy-five years old, Shoghi Effendi announced that he was a Hand of the Cause of God. Although he was elderly, he travelled to many countries to meet with the Bahá'ís, and he gave talks at hundreds of meetings. He was not very tall, but he had a powerful voice, and people loved to hear his stories. The stories they liked to hear most of all were about when he was in the presence of Bahá'u'lláh. When they looked into Mr Samandarí's eyes, they would remember that his eyes had gazed on the face of Bahá'u'lláh, and this made them feel close to Bahá'u'lláh too.

Shoghi Effendi loved Mr Samandarí very much and said he was like a shining lamp among the Bahá'í teachers.

40

Pilgrims

Pilgrims came from all over the world to pray in the Shrines of the Báb and Bahá'u'lláh. When new pilgrims arrived, Shoghi Effendi would greet them warmly, saying, "Welcome! Welcome!" One of them said that Shoghi Effendi embraced him with such tenderness that he felt he was in the arms of all the mothers in the world.

When a new pilgrim arrived, Shoghi Effendi would invite him or her to sit in the seat of honour at the head of the table. Shoghi Effendi would then share news from around the world or a plan he was working on, and sometimes he became so happy he forgot to eat!

One Holy Day, the anniversary of the Ascension of Bahá'u'lláh, Shoghi Effendi took the pilgrims to Bahjí. It was evening when they arrived, and everyone sat outside the Shrine of Bahá'u'lláh in the peaceful, tree-lined garden. Prayers were chanted and passages read from Bahá'u'lláh's beautiful Writings. Then Shoghi Effendi gave a talk about Bahá'u'lláh.

As it grew dark, the shapes of the trees stood out against the moonlit sky. Some of the trees had leaves that looked like hands on the end of their branches. They looked as though they were lifting their hands in prayer and all of the garden felt holy.

Shoghi Effendi led the way to the Shrine, and everyone followed. He anointed the friends with perfume of roses. Then they stepped, one by one, from the dark garden into the glorious light of the Shrine.

41

Pioneers

'Abdu'l-Bahá had written some important letters called Tablets of the Divine Plan. In these letters, He told the Bahá'ís to leave their homes and travel to other countries to tell people about Bahá'u'lláh.

Shoghi Effendi also encouraged the friends to travel to different parts of the world and share the Bahá'í teachings with others. He said that the Bahá'í Faith is for everyone, and everyone must have the chance to hear about it. It does not matter where people live, what colour they are, what language they speak, whether they are young or old, girls or boys, rich or poor. Everyone, said Shoghi Effendi, is important.

He gave the Bahá'ís a teaching plan, based on 'Abdu'l-Bahá's Tablets. It was called the Ten Year Crusade. By the end of the ten years, in 1963, the Bahá'í Faith had spread to nearly every country and island in the world.

When Bahá'ís left their homes to live somewhere else so they could teach the Faith, Shoghi Effendi called them pioneers. Because of these pioneers, even people living on tiny islands in the middle of oceans, in mud huts in the middle of jungles, and in igloos near the north pole, heard about Bahá'u'lláh and became Bahá'ís.

A seventeen-year-old boy wanted to be a pioneer, but everyone thought he was too young. When Shoghi Effendi heard about him, he wrote to the Bahá'í community where the boy lived and asked the Local Spiritual Assembly there to help the young man to pioneer. An old lady who was unable to walk also wanted to pioneer. Her family and friends thought she was far too ill and old to travel to another country. But Shoghi Effendi encouraged her to go. He knew she wanted to do something special for Bahá'u'lláh and that it would make her happy.

Sometimes whole families pioneered. Children who had been born in Persia found themselves going to school in Africa. And children who were born in America found themselves living on islands near Australia.

42

Roses

A pioneer who lived near the North Pole came on pilgrimage. Shoghi Effendi asked about her life among the friendly Inuit people, in a land covered in ice and snow, where very few trees or flowers grew.

The believer told Shoghi Effendi that some of the Inuit who lived in the far north of the world did not always understand some of the words in the Writings of Bahá'u'lláh. For example, because it was so cold in their land, roses did not grow there and most of the people had never seen one, so they had no idea what they were like.

Bahá'u'lláh often speaks about roses. In one of the Hidden Words He says:

"O FRIEND!

In the garden of thy heart plant naught but the rose of love...."

So this was quite a problem.

Shoghi Effendi did not say anything at the time. But when the pilgrimage came to an end he gave the pioneer a gift for the Inuit Bahá'ís. It was something that would help them know what a lovely smell roses have.

He gave her a small bottle of perfume of roses!

43

Beginning the Arc

Shoghi Effendi had already built graceful white marble monuments over the graves of the Holy Family on Mount Carmel. These graves are where some members of Bahá'u'lláh's Family are buried: His wife, His daughter, and one of His sons. 'Abdu'l-Bahá's wife is also buried there. Shoghi Effendi said that these holy graves would be in the middle of an arc made of five important buildings which would be built on the mountain one day.

Shoghi Effendi built the first of these buildings. It is a museum, called the International Archives, where important and interesting items which had belonged to Bahá'u'lláh and the Báb and members of the Holy Family are kept. These include a photograph of Bahá'u'lláh and a painting of the Báb, letters they had written, pens they had used, and some of their clothes. But before these precious things could be displayed for people to see, Shoghi Effendi needed to build the museum.

Forty-six white pillars were carved from quarries in Italy. And nearly eight thousand blue-green tiles were specially made in Holland for the roof. It took seventeen ships to bring all the pillars and the rest of the materials to Haifa.

In one of the walls, Shoghi Effendi put a tall window made of different coloured glass. It is very beautiful. Every afternoon the sun shines on the coloured window and fills the hall inside with dazzling red and blue and yellow light.

Most precious of all, when the Bahá'ís come on pilgrimage to the Holy Land, they can go inside the lovely International Archives building and kneel before the holy pictures of the Báb and Bahá'u'lláh.

44

The Passing of Shoghi Effendi

It was the autumn of 1957. When the International Archives building was finished, Shoghi Effendi and Rúhíyyih Khánum travelled to London to buy furniture to put inside it. Chandeliers were needed to light the large hall, and cabinets were needed to display the articles that had belonged to the Holy Family.

It was cold and wet in London, quite different from the warm weather in Haifa. Shoghi Effendi had just finished buying everything he needed for the Archives building when he fell ill with flu. A doctor came and gave him medicine, and after a few days Shoghi Effendi seemed to be getting better. He was even well enough to work on a large map he was making which showed all the places in the world where there were Bahá'ís.

But Shoghi Effendi was not getting better. His heart was tired from all the hard work he had been doing for so many years. One night, as he peacefully slept in his bed, his heart stopped beating. Beloved Shoghi Effendi had died.

As soon as they heard the news, Bahá'ís from countries all over the world travelled to London. A lovely spot was found among tall trees in a cemetery on the edge of London, and this is where Shoghi Effendi was buried.

Hundreds of people, including children, gathered for the funeral. They lovingly laid their gifts of flowers on Shoghi Effendi's grave and prayers were recited and chanted. The believers were sad because Shoghi Effendi's life in this world had ended, but they were happy that his soul was with Bahá'u'lláh and 'Abdu'l-Bahá in the glorious Abhá Kingdom.

45

A Spiritual Crusade

At first the Bahá'ís did not know what to do when Shoghi Effendi died. It seemed that there was nobody to guide them. But there were still the Hands of the Cause of God and they reminded the friends of the Plan that Shoghi Effendi had made. This Plan was the Ten Year Crusade, and because of it, people all over the world were hearing about the teachings of Bahá'u'lláh for the first time. The Hands of the Cause said that at the end of the ten years, the first Universal House of Justice would be elected and this is what would look after the Bahá'ís in the future.

One of the Bahá'ís who had taken part in the Ten Year Crusade was a small girl named Sáteh. At the beginning of the Ten Year Crusade, Shoghi Effendi had asked Sáteh's father and mother to leave Persia and pioneer to Africa, which they did, taking their three children with them.

When Sáteh and her brothers and parents arrived in Africa they did not have much money. But they did not mind. The children went to the village school with the African children and their parents held meetings in their small house to tell people about Bahá'u'lláh.

Many other Bahá'ís also left their homes and pioneered. And people who had been Christians or Muslims or Buddhists or Hindus or Zoroastrians or Jews, or had no religion at all, heard the teachings of Bahá'u'lláh and became Bahá'ís. People who believed in African and Red Indian religions also believed. They ıll knew that Bahá'u'lláh was the Messenger of God they were vaiting for. The teachings of their own religions had said He vould come one day to bring peace to the world.

In 1957, which is when Shoghi Effendi died and his soul left his world to go to the next, four and a half years of the Crusade ıad already passed by. There were five and a half years to go, ınd plenty of work to do as people in some countries still had ıot heard about Bahá'u'lláh and the new teachings from God.

In 1963 the Crusade ended. And the first Bahá'í World Congress vas held to celebrate.

The year 1963 was also important for another reason. It was exactly one hundred years before, in 1863, when Bahá'u'lláh first said He was the Manifestation of God everyone was waiting for.

46

The Celebration

Thousands of Bahá'ís began to arrive in London to celebrate at the first Bahá'í World Congress. They came in boats and planes and trains and cars and buses. Inuits came from the snowy north and Aboriginals came from sunny Australia. Bolivians in ponchos and tall coloured hats arrived from mountain villages in South America. And Peruvian Indians came from villages deep in the rain forests. Bahá'ís came from Persia and India, Europe and America, Arabia and Africa, Japan, Canada and Asia, and some countries which most people had never heard of before.

Sáteh came from Africa with her parents and brothers. She looked in amazement at the seven thousand smiling faces in the Royal Albert Hall in London, where the celebration was being held. She had never seen so many Bahá'ís gathered together before. Many of them were wearing their national dress – brightly coloured clothes which they wore in their own countries. They looked like beautiful flowers in the garden of God.

How happy Shoghi Effendi must have been in the Abhá Kingdom to know that so many people from different countries were gathered together in unity.

How happy the friends were when they thought of Shoghi Effendi and how it was because of his Ten Year Crusade that so many of them had heard about Bahá'u'lláh.

Dear Shoghi Effendi, whose eyes were full of kindness and light, who had signed his letters "Your true brother, Shoghi" and said, "I will continue to pray for all of you from the depths of my heart."

Sources

'Abdu'l-Bahá, *Will and Testament of 'Abdu'l-Bahá* (New Delhi Bahá'í Publishing Trust, 1999)

Balyuzi, H. M., *'Abdu'l-Bahá* (Oxford: George Ronald, 1971)

Faizí, Abu'l-Qásím, *Milly: a tribute to Amelia Collins* (Oxford George Ronald, 1977)

Giachery, Ugo, *Shoghi Effendi, Recollections* (Oxford: Georg Ronald, 1973)

Rúhíyyih Rabbani, *The Priceless Pearl* (London: Bahá'í Publishin Trust, 1969)

Samandarí, Tarázu'lláh, *Moments with Bahá'u'lláh* (Los Angeles Kalimát Press, 1995)

Shoghi Effendi, *Unfolding Destiny* (London: Bahá'í Publishin Trust, 1981)

Taherzadeh, Adib, *The Covenant of Bahá'u'lláh* (Oxford: Georg Ronald, 1992)

Yazdi, Ali M., *Blessings Beyond Measure* (Wilmette: Bahá' Publishing Trust, 1988)